RECEIVING THE MARROW

Teachings On Dogen by Soto Zen Women Priests

EDITED BY

EIDO FRANCES CARNEY

Temple Ground Press

3248 39th Way NE

Olympia, WA 98506

www.OlympiaZenCenter.org/TempleGroundPress

Copyright © 2012 Temple Ground Press

Temple Ground publishes works that further the teachings of Soto Zen Buddhism.

Library of Congress Cataloging-in-Publication Data

EAN-13: 978-0-9855651-0-7
ISBN-10: 0985565101

Library of Congress Control Number: 2012938723
Temple Ground Press, Olympia WA

Dedicated To

Our Great Teacher and Founder of Soto Zen Eihei Dogen
and to the Dharma Transmitted successors
who saw and gave everything to everyone

Contents

Introduction Eido Frances Carney   vii

Brief Biography of Zen Master Dogen   xvii

A Note on Formatting   xxxi

Dancing the Dharma *Bendowa* Teijo Munnich   1

One Bright Jewel *Ikka no Myoju* Shotai De La Rosa   15

Not Doing Evils *Shoaku Makusa* Seisen Saunders   37

Dogen's Seven Arguments for Empowering Zen Women
Raihaitokuzui Grace Jill Schireson   57

Astride the Highest Mountain: Dogen's Being/Time,
A Practitioner's Guide *Uji* Shinshu Roberts   69

Great Realization *Daigo* Byakuren Judith Ragir   99

Polishing a Tile, Actualizing a Mirror *Zazenshin*
Josho Pat Phelan   125

The True Human Body *Shinjingakudo*
Shosan Victoria Austin   139

On the Moon as One's Excellent Nature *Tsuki*
Eido Frances Carney   163

All Beings Sing the Song of Dharma *Mujo Seppo*
Jisho Warner   185

Udumbara Flower *Udonge* Jan Chozen Bays   207

Works Consulted for the Introduction and Brief
Biography of Dogen   219

Glossary of Terms Used in the Essays   221

Contributor Biographies   229

Introduction

The notion for this collection came out of a dinner conversation during a meeting of the Association of Soto Zen Buddhists in Los Angeles. I sat at a dinner table with a small group of women priests who began to discuss the issues and challenges of teaching Dogen's *Shobogenzo*, a monumental work of deep spiritual intensity. Listening to their insights on Dogen's teachings, I regretted that more people could not hear their commentaries, their insights and sound scholarship. When pressed to answer why their essays were not in print, they responded with a vague list of resistances. They expressed time limitations in the effort it takes to move writing from manuscript to published work. The call to attend to the management of a temple is a demanding and all consuming vocation. They may have felt their work was inadequate for publication. There may have been a hesitancy to leave the comfort and privacy of the temple and jump into the arena of a critical and discerning public where few Soto Zen women priests have gone.

In spite of the resistances, the challenge to go forward persisted and a proposal for a book collection was issued to Soto Zen women priests and many responded positively. It seemed an obvious venture because of the dearth of women's commentary on Dogen's teachings.

Several well-known Buddhist publishers refused the project because in their view, women's equality has already been achieved so women are no longer specifically cultivated in publishing. They asked why men weren't present in this collection. Another reason for rejection was that anthologies do not sell. This is not true in the academic arena where the university publishers continue to produce Buddhist anthologies with only male authors. Although they declined to publish this collection, the Buddhist publishers nevertheless thought the project was a fine idea and deserved to come to print.

From the vantage point of hearing women's voices teaching on Dogen, we cared little about sales and profit, an obvious interest for a publisher. Our concern in publishing women's voices is so future Zen students may be able to trace the history and articulation of women teachers of this century. Each generation exploring the lineage will ask how did earlier teachers function in the world, how did they teach, how did they come forward and become visible, how did they lead? Since we ourselves are disappointed by limited evidence in researching our own lost sisters, we feel an obligation to care for the future by offering our voices now so we do not create an absence on which future claims of exclusion may be based. We are responsible for ourselves, and we have a duty to see that we do not generate wars of gender and discrimination into the future. To that end, we must stand visibly in the very equality that Dogen Zenji declares when he says, "Do not discriminate between men and women. This is the most wondrous principle of the Buddha Way." The equality we enjoy today must be cared for, fostered, never abused, and preserved as the foundation of future practitioners.

Women live with an essentially unrecorded history; we have only a brief women's literature to which we refer. In the history of the world's religions, we have a mere cupful of spiritual texts written by, or about women. Throughout history it has been rare to find women of any religion who stood on their own spiritual authority, rather than an authority lent to them by men. Privilege prevented women from achieving legitimacy without a man's confirmation and promotion. In coming to Dogen now, we don't rise to demonstrate our full capacities because Dogen says so, we rise, because we ourselves understand, by right of our practice-experience and spiritual authority in the Buddha Dharma, that Awakening does not make distinctions. Thus, we stand side by side with Dogen Zenji in confirmation of his teachings.

This collection then is not a feminist treatise but an extension of the right and just equality that belongs to all sentient beings. It takes at least ten years of actual teaching to become a teacher, and it takes many more years of studying *Shobogenzo* or any of Dogen's writings to be competent enough to stand with Dogen and attempt to explain and explicate his intentions. Since many of our Soto Zen women priests received Dharma Transmission in the 1990's, we have only recently come into our own as teachers. There is the danger of arrogance if we take up Dogen too early without stable roots in the soil of Dharma. The seed that has been planted needs to properly settle and be confident that it is not promoting misunderstandings of what Dogen intended. In Japan, the convention is that younger priests, at least under 60, should not take up teaching *Shobogenzo* because they are not seasoned and mature enough to meet the spiritual giant that is Dogen Zenji. Great deference is paid to the Founder of Soto Zen.

This collection of essays includes women whose teaching would not be heard today if Soto Zen did not have an egalitarian founder such as Dogen Zenji. He set the stage for women to come forward and stand as equals in a clerical world that had rejected them as full members of the institution. The overwhelming evidence is that Dogen welcomed women into Soto Zen. Uses of language that indicate Dogen's inclusiveness of women in practice are scattered throughout *Shobogenzo*. On occasion, rather than using an obvious masculine expression, Dogen might use the neutral expression "someone" to describe a monk, which would seem to indicate he is meaning to include women monks as well as lay men and lay women practitioners. The earliest fascicle *Bendowa*, "On the Endeavor of the Way," written in 1231, serves as a preamble to his view. Dogen says, "The ancestors have said in their teaching, 'When it comes to realizing the Buddha Dharma, make no distinction between men and women, or between nobles and commoners.'" He asks, "Who among humans and heavenly beings could be excluded from Realization?"

The strongest affirmation of women is in the fascicle *Raihaitokuzui*, "Receiving the Marrow by Bowing," written at Koshoji Monastery in April, 1240. Here, Dogen is even more explicit and at his most intentional. The *Raihaitokuzui* is in two parts. In the first section Dogen teaches that we should be willing and open to learning the Buddha Dharma from women, men, or animals, whether or not they are alive or dead.

In the second part, written six months later in October, he takes up various questions about the importance of being able to learn from women and having a woman as a teacher. In this second section, he is more deeply critical of negative attitudes toward women, and he uses very assertive language to make radical statements on behalf of women. But for reasons that we truly do not know, this second section, certainly written by Dogen, was kept under lock and key at Eiheiji and only revealed in a much later version of the *Shobogenzo*.

We know that Dogen brought back from China, more enlightened attitudes toward women whom he witnessed leading practice, encountered in various temples, and in the literature, and he attempted to implant these egalitarian views in his native Japan. Indeed, he likely tried to influence the state with notions of equality. He knew on return to Japan that he would invite women into his Sangha, which he did do. He had numerous women students, as did his successors, although Dogen did not ordain any women. Neither did he go so far as to order equality in the Zendo, where women sat in a lower-status position, so Dogen was not without contradiction in the matter of discrimination. But Japan is an island nation and not easily influenced by outside views. It does not share a land border with any other culture. It had no real intercultural traffic to inform and percolate through its social structures.

It's hard to know whether Dogen, discovering himself in the thicket of male privilege, found so much negative resistance from his fellow priests that he chose to keep the second section of *Raihaitokuzui* hidden; or, whether others, fearing women might gain privilege in Buddhism or in society itself, suppressed the writing after Dogen's death. We can see through world history that the greatest resistance to change is found in the system of privilege. Dogen, as a social reformer, in spite of all his insight into equality, confronted an unyielding system and an orchestrated culture. He may simply have chosen his battles. Throughout history, spiritual truth has been discarded in favor of continuing a system of privilege because privilege is the last thing that anyone will forfeit, in spite of the suffering caused. This is still true in the 21st Century and both men and women are culpable in maintaining a matrix of privilege regarding gender, race, age, disability, ethnicity, sexual orientation, and the concomitant suffering caused by a global system of privilege.

I have no doubt that in speaking for women Dogen means to speak against all forms of discrimination. In place of women, substitute the name of any group of lesser privilege and we arrive at the same teaching. Dogen writes: "Should you despise women (or a race) because you think that in ancient times they have committed some offense, then you must despise all bodhisattvas as well. Or should you despise women (or a race) because you think that at some later date they will surely commit some offense, then you must despise all bodhisattvas who have given rise to the intention to realize Buddhahood. If you despise women (or a race) in any such ways, you must despise every single person, so how can Buddha Dharma be actualized?" Dogen asserts very clearly that exclusionary practices against women are cultural biases and are unsupported and unjustified by the Buddha Dharma. He says that no one should believe discriminatory practices to be what Truth is.

Now, as I mentioned, we truly can't know whether or not it was Dogen who suppressed the stronger statements on women's equality, and we can't know how our evolution might have been different for both men and women had Dogen's teachings on equality had a more sweeping effect beginning in the 13th century. What we do have is a "post-existentialist Dogen" translated fully in the 21st Century who illuminates equality of all peoples and who seeks to rid the culture of long-held negative attitudes that are against the spirit of Buddhism. We can, and we must, in this century, follow Dogen's prescriptions for pure practice; in fact, we have the honor of lifting him and ourselves out of the constraints and dilemmas of all areas of privilege, and manifesting what Dogen might have wished for in his own time, influencing culture as far and wide as he hoped.

Most of us in the English speaking world could not know Dogen and his Awakened spirit without the many who have given their lives to the important work of translation. Through their effort and scholarship, the gates of Dharma to all English speaking peoples have been opened. Anyone who has read even a small portion of Dogen's writings can grasp the difficulty and challenge to translate 13th Century Japanese into modern English. We can only bow deeply in awe and gratitude.

Now that we have the platform to speak and the brilliant translations with which to work, we have still the challenge to meet Dogen on his own ground. This is a formidable task. Who can say that they actually grasp Dogen? The closer we come the more we seem to slip away from nailing the point. It takes some modicum of courage to stand on the edge of the cliff and take the dangerous, tomb-stoning leap. Yet we take it up because it is fraught with tension, the same kind of tension that we engage in a koan. As we know, hesitation is what makes us afraid. Just as work on a koan opens the heart-mind, I have no doubt that for the contributors the writing of these essays expanded their sense of being, and the sense of being with Dogen. It is this engagement with him that makes us ever more respectful of the immeasurable and profound nature of his life. Some of these fascicles of Dogen have not been considered in print prior to this collection. We are wandering in a field beyond the most considered texts to look at a wider variety of his writings. Wherever we go, Dogen remains relentless in requiring the best of our clear and bright minds in responding to *The True Treasury of the Eye of the Dharma*. Or, perhaps it's better to say that to be with him requires our deepest and most authentic practice.

While this collection of essays is a gesture of gratitude to Dogen for his spiritual Truth, we would be remiss to not pay honor to two other important ancients: the first woman of the Monastic Order and the Mother of Buddhism, Our Great Teacher Mahapajapati, and Ananda who stood up for women even when Shakyamuni denied them. Both Mahapajapati and Ananda were saints far ahead of their time. Mahapajapati fought for democratic rule, took in the weary and infirm, the dislocated and discarded, the invisible among the invisible in the caste system, and transformed their lives into the dignity of spiritual kinship and order. Ananda stuck his neck out and interceded with the Buddha for women's acceptance into the monastic order. We can imagine that Ananda must have been repudiated by his Sangha brothers and reprimanded by the Buddha. The Sangha considered Ananda to be somewhat slow and unworthy, yet, the nuns respected him more highly than any of his brother monks. Because of the courage of these two saints, we have women in the monastic order from the time of the Buddha.

The collection contributes to our Soto Zen literature by bringing forward seasoned voices of priest-teachers in their kinship with Dogen, interpreting him as a clear dynamic and force of spirit for the 21st century. The essays are an homage to Dogen, an implicit expression of gratitude to our translators, and a tribute to women and men standing together teaching side by side, supporting one another fully and equally in the Buddha Dharma.

With deepest thankfulness to the priest-teachers who offer their wisdom in this celebration of Dogen Zenji. Our voices are varied and are our own as we go forward finding our Way, step by step as teachers and leaders of spiritual communities. Thank you to the many who offered counsel and wisdom to the contributors, and to me, by way of editing, collecting, encouraging, and moving this spiritual collaboration into living form. Such generosity is deeply acknowledged.

Eido Frances Carney

A Brief Biography of
Zen Master Dogen

Formative Years 1200 - 1223

The Japanese socio-political climate during Dogen's early years was complex and turbulent. He was born in Kyoto in 1200 to an aristocratic family rife with ambition for political prominence. After his father died when Dogen was three, other family members sought to adopt him and use his family position to reestablish their own social and governmental influence, but his mother protected him from such a fate. In 1207, his mother died, and his elder half brother, referred to in the history books as his 'stepfather,' raised him. Dogen's education would have included the classics, writing, literature and any of the particular studies important to aristocratic life. He had a highly developed poetic sensibility and a predilection for language and linguistics. By the age of nine he was already reading advanced Buddhist texts and thinking about the impermanence of life.

When Dogen was 13, he ran away from the mountain villa where he lived to an uncle's hermitage at the foot of Mt. Hiei near Kyoto. Dogen was able to convince his uncle, Monk Ryokan, that he was sincere in his desire to renounce the world and become a novice. He recounted how his mother, on her deathbed, urged him to take the robe, to turn toward the Buddha's teachings and to live a monastic life. Now he knew it was time to take the robe and the monastic life was the correct path. The sincerity of his words rang true to Monk Ryokan. In 1213, Dogen shaved his head and received preliminary Precepts in the Tendai School of Buddhism. The Tendai School was a synthesis of various Chinese teachings, Zen, Esoteric Buddhism of the Shingon Sect, and the Vinaya School. The primary work of monks in this formalistic atmosphere was to copy sutras, holy texts.

Because of a split between leaders in the Tendai School, the political atmosphere at Mt. Hiei turned hostile, even before Dogen arrived, and many monks became warriors to defend their properties and territories. Much of this turmoil was driven by an aristocratic dominance in the hierarchies of clerical life. While earlier Mt. Hiei had been a center for Buddhist education, it now evolved into a place of active hostility. Monks disillusioned by the fighting and political jostling left Mt. Hiei and some of them travelled to China to explore the Chinese Buddhism that was influencing the Japanese.

During his training at Mt. Hiei, Dogen developed a sense of grave doubt concerning a teaching of the Buddha. The Buddha had said, "All sentient beings everywhere have Buddha-nature. The Tatagatha exists eternally and is without change." Dogen asked if this teaching were true, then why should people seek enlightenment and engage in practice to pursue enlightenment? He did not question the original enlightenment, but rather the praxis, the concomitant activities by which humans demonstrate that enlightenment. Why should we practice any kind of spiritual activity if we are already enlightened? Dogen went about asking teachers to answer this question, but he was dissatisfied with the answers he received. He was just fourteen when this doubt nearly consumed him.

Dogen transferred to several temples during this developmental stage and was said to have briefly met Eisai, the founder of the Lin-chi (Rinzai) School. Eisai remained a member of the Tendai Sect yet hoped to establish his own teachings and simultaneously revitalize Tendai by sharing what he experienced during his training in China. Eisai had studied at Ching-te Monastery on T'ien-t'ung Mountain where he received Dharma Transmission in the Lin-chi lineage. After Eisai's death, the priest Myozen succeeded him, and it was with Myozen at temple Kennin-ji, that Dogen continued to probe his deep, unresolved question. His uncle, Ryokan, also died, and thus Dogen essentially concluded his association with Mt. Hiei and became a disciple of Myozen.

Dogen was eager to sail to China in search of a teacher who could resolve his question. The travel ban was lifted after the Jokyu War, the war between emperors, but Myozen was faced with the fatal illness of a former teacher on Mt. Hiei who wanted Myozen to assist during his dying process. Dogen argued that the search for the true teacher and the Buddha Dharma took precedence, so Myozen agreed and made the decision to sail. In 1223, Myozen and Dogen with two other monks travelled to Kyushu by way of the Inland Sea, then boarded a merchant vessel for the trip across the terrifying waters of the China Sea.

Pilgrimage to China 1223 - 1227

Once in China, Myozen travelled directly to Ching-te Monastery while Dogen remained on board the merchant ship for three months, although we don't exactly know why. It is possible that he didn't have the required clerical immigration documents to enter China. During this time, Dogen encountered an old monk, the chief cook at a temple, who had come a good distance to the ship to buy mushrooms from Japan. Dogen was surprised that the old monk did his own shopping and thought surely he should have an underling to do this work. Dogen invited the monk to take a rest and stay the night onboard, but the old monk replied that he had to return to his monastery so as not to cause any disruption, that he was the chief cook and cooking was his Way of practice. Besides, he hadn't received permission to be out overnight. He told Dogen that he, Dogen, didn't understand the nature of words or discipline if he could ask the old monk to so easily abandon his brothers in the monastery and forget his work as chief cook. He invited Dogen to visit his temple someday and study there. Dogen was greatly impressed with this exchange as he began to sense there was more to seeking enlightenment and the Way of practice than his own intellection; that Zen practice included all the expressions of daily life.

Sometime after his encounter with the old cook, Dogen went to T'ien-t'ung Mountain to see Myozen. While there, he experienced several other formative moments. At the finish of Zazen one morning, a monk next to him put his monk's robe, *kasaya,* on his head and chanted before wearing it. Dogen was overcome since he had never seen any monk do this in Japan even though he had read about it in the *Agama Sutra.* He was filled with joy and weeping with gratitude that he had come to China to experience this while at the same time feeling deep remorse for his countrymen who had no opportunity to witness the beauty of this practice.

Dogen vowed at that moment: "With compassion for my fellow countrymen I will, unworthy though I am, become an heir to Buddhism, a right receiver of the true Way, and teach them the Law that was correctly transmitted by the Buddhas and patriarchs together with the *kasaya.*"

In another encounter, Dogen spotted an old monk drying mushrooms in the garden under a very hot sun. Dogen asked the old monk why he didn't direct younger monks to do this laborious work, or else wait until it wasn't so hot, but the old monk said that if he didn't do it now, when should he do it? Startled by such great devotion, Dogen realized the importance of physical labor as an expression of Dharma. Later, the old monk whom he'd met onboard the ship came to the temple to see Dogen while on his way to Szechuan. Another exchange with the chief cook taught Dogen that great effort was the means to bring about pure meditation, or that fulfillment in work and discipline were one and the same. After all, Dogen had been raised in a privileged atmosphere and had little experience of hard, physical work. This encounter influenced Dogen throughout his whole life. His instructions in the care of the kitchen and those working in the kitchen, and not just the chief cook, were some of his most influential teachings in the monastic code. He wrote: "These (instructions) are the lifeblood of the Buddhas and Ancestors and the Eye of patch-robed monks....Only the disciples of Buddha have been able to Transmit them. O you who are senior officers of the Kitchen Hall, discern them well and do not let them be lost!"

Pilgrimages to various temples were also part of Dogen's experience in his first years in China during which time he viewed several documents of succession, proof of one's lineage from Shakyamuni Buddha to the present through face-to-face transmission. Dogen was deeply moved at seeing these documents, but he was still in search of the true teacher. He was unimpressed with the teaching methodologies he observed, which were primarily in the Lin-chi lineage. He decided to return to Myozen and T'ien-t'ung Mountain with the idea of returning to Japan and abandoning his search, which began to seem fruitless. Another exchange with an old monk along the road informed Dogen that a new abbot, Tiantong Rujing (1163-1228, Tendo Nyojo in Japanese) now served at T'ien-t'ung Mountain and that Rujing was surely the finest living teacher in all of China.

Dogen went straightaway and in his first exchanges with Rujing, in the Ts'ao-tung (hereafter using Japanese: Soto) School, recognized Rujing as his true teacher. Surely Rujing recognized in Dogen a true aspiration for enlightenment. Although Dogen had become disenchanted with the methodologies of the Lin-chi teachers, he did not choose Rujing because of a sectarian difference. It was a case of each recognizing Buddha in the other and the perfect trust that came as a result of that recognition. Dogen stresses this nonsectarian view a number of times in his later writings. "Before I had done my respectful bows to my late Master, an Old Buddha, I had already aimed at thoroughly exploring the so-called 'deeper principles of the five sects'. After I had done my respectful bows to my late Master, the Old Buddha, I clearly understood that 'the five sects' was just an arbitrary name." Dogen thus became a student in Rujing's monastery.

A month or so later, Myozen sadly fell ill and died. Dogen would later bring Myozen's ashes, said to contain sacred relics, back to Japan, where he entrusted the ashes to one of Myozen's students.

Practice at Rujing's monastery was severe. Meditation was emphasized as the primary activity and the day began with washing the face at 1 a.m. Other temples Dogen visited did not have such rigorous schedules nor had the teachers placed such importance upon Zazen, sitting meditation, as did Rujing. Rujing himself kept the difficult schedule. Dogen quotes the Old Master as being singleminded and steadfast in the practice of Zazen, *Shikantaza*, just sitting. "I always felt," said Rujing, "that I would like to sit upon the Diamond Seat until it split, for this was the outcome I was seeking. There were times when the flesh on my buttocks would blister and split open. At such times I all the more took delight in sitting in meditation....Accordingly, I am Abbot of this mountain monastery so that I may counsel those who come here and Transmit the Way to them for the sake of all beings. Otherwise, my old friends, where could the Buddha Dharma be found and what would It be like?"

This unswerving and indefatigable spirit of Rujing infused Dogen with the considerable energy to press through. In other words, Dogen had finally met a teacher who could meet his own indefatigability and determination to Awaken. While Dogen was a man of great independence, he gave total trust and obedience to his teacher, and Rujing admired this quality in Dogen. No matter how exhausted the monks became, Rujing would encourage them to remain awake insisting that such discipline was the hallmark of one on the Buddha's path. Dogen himself was prepared to die and determined that he would remain awake in Zazen even if he were to be inflicted with some dread disease. It was this absolute conviction and faith in the Buddha's Awakening and in each one's potential for realization that enveloped Dogen's body and mind.

In the tautness of this atmosphere, as the mythic story goes, Dogen came to realization. While sitting Zazen during the early morning hours of a long retreat, the monk next to Dogen fell asleep. Rujing noticed the monk bobbing on his cushion and yelled, "When sitting Zazen, it is necessary to cast off body and mind. How can you dare to fall asleep?" At that moment, when Dogen heard those words, he was filled with extraordinary light and his entire being was overcome with limitless joy. Later in the morning, Dogen went to Rujing's private rooms and offered incense. Rujing came to him and asked why he was making this offering. Dogen answered, "Body and mind are cast off!" Rujing looked into Dogen's being and said, "Body and mind are cast off; cast off are body and mind." In so speaking, Rujing completely recognized and acknowledged Dogen's authentic nature.

Now, at last, Dogen was transformed as he realized the answer to his search in the profound experience of Buddha Nature. He realized the essential non-dualism of practice and enlightenment, of his being in the world and taking action in the world. Since his entire being was the original enlightenment, spiritual practice in and through Zazen was the true and perfect expression of Buddha Nature. Dogen in his later writings attended very closely to the meaning and importance of Buddha Nature. He asserted through and through that sentient beings have, are not separate from, are fully endowed with, and are completely Buddha Nature. "What sentient beings experience as existing both within and outside themselves will, therefore, be their 'having Buddha Nature through and through. It goes beyond the Skin and Flesh, Bones and Marrow that are directly Transmitted from Master to disciple, one-to-one, because one has already acquired the Master's Skin and

Flesh, Bones and Marrow. You need to realize right now that the existence, which is had through and through by Buddha Nature, is beyond the existence of 'existing versus not existing.' 'Having it through and through' is the Buddha's term. It is the Tongue of Buddhas. It is the Eye of the Buddhas and Ancestors. It is the Nose of mendicant monks." Rujing thus Transmitted to Dogen affirmation of his enlightenment and the lineage of the authentic Transmission of the Bodhisattva Precepts unbroken from Shakyamuni Buddha through the entire Indian and Chinese ancestral line. Rujing had emphasized the importance of a direct face-to-face Transmission, dropping off body and mind, and now Dogen had the Treasure of his true spiritual inheritance. The year was 1225.

Two years later in 1227, Dogen announced his wish to return to Japan. Rujing was said to have bestowed upon Dogen the Robe of Fu-yung Tao-k'ai (Fuyo Dokai 1043-1118, an earlier teacher in the Soto lineage), several sacred texts, and a portrait of his teacher. Rujing encouraged Dogen to wear the Robe and to spread the teachings of the Soto inheritance. Thus Dogen made preparations to return to his homeland, carrying the invisible Treasure of the Eye-to Eye Transmission and the heart of a true Bodhisattva.

Rujing died in 1228, a profound yet humble teacher who had helped to take Dogen beyond any traces of arrogance and intellect. Rujing resisted fame and notoriety, and saw the shortcomings of his contemporary teachers yet eschewed any sense of sectarianism and separation from the various schools in Buddhism. Rujing, profoundly confident in the Dharma, offered a highly disciplined practice with emphasis on single-minded and intense sitting meditation, Zazen. The implication of this for Dogen's enlightenment and for the teaching he would transmit to Japan could not be more essential, for it became the very core of Dogen's teaching and the foundation of Soto Zen in Japan.

The Way in Japan 1227 – 1252

Once back in Japan, Dogen returned to Kenninji where he had practiced with Myozen and where he stayed for another three years. He felt the weight of the Bodhisattva mission that came with his great vow to save beings from suffering, and to promote the Dharma, a natural outcome of his enlightenment experience. In the somewhat chaotic atmosphere of Kenninji, and in the shadow of the politics of Mt. Hiei, Dogen began to clarify the direction of his teachings. His first writing, *Fukanzazengi*, the basic practice of Zazen he wrote: "The Buddhas and patriarchs, both in this world and that, in India and in China, have all preserved the Buddha-mind and enhanced Zen training. You should therefore devote yourself exclusively to and be completely absorbed in the practice of Zazen." As his influence grew, it became clear that he had to venture on his own and develop the practice, which was now the central aim of his life. He took over an abandoned temple called An'yoin in Fukakusa, south of Kyoto, where he wrote another important formative text called Bendowa, which together with Fukanzazengi became the mainspring of his teachings.

Yet another move in 1233, also in Fukakusa, to Kannon-doriinji, produced ten years of intense development. For the rest of Dogen's life, his shining disciple, Koun Ejo, well educated in Buddhism and mature practice in other sects, devoted himself to his teacher to begin the spread of Soto Zen in Japan. In these years, 1233-1243, Dogen wrote forty-four chapters of

Shobogenzo, The Treasury of the True Eye of the Dharma, established the foundations of daily monastic practice, enlarged the temple by building a new monk's hall to house his followers in this new expression of Buddhist practice. The temple was renamed Kosho-horinji, and Dogen formed the essential design of the monastic grounds to include not only the meditation hall for the practice of Zazen and location where monks slept and kept their small belongings, but also the Dharma hall for the practice of ceremony, and the monk's hall to include kitchen practice and education. During this developmental phase, Dogen's influence was growing.

Dogen's renown spread as he opened the practice to include lay people, both men and women, and his teachings and practice became clearly distinguished from other schools of Buddhism. Dogen's form of Zen was unique in Japan and he felt the importance of establishing a pure Zen, not inferior or superior, but authentic in form and practice. This brought notoriety to Dogen and it did not always sit well with the other traditional schools around him. In 1243, Hatano Yoshishige, a feudal lord, disciple and primary patron, offered Dogen property in Echizen in the north of Japan, to move his monastic center to the less politically entangled mountain country. Dogen's teacher Rujing had cautioned him to stay clear of the center of cities, to avoid association with governmental ministers, and to live in the quiet of mountains where one can focus closely on practice.

While this move made sense to Dogen for many reasons, some of which were aesthetic and some political discretion, it profoundly changed the focus of his Zen from one of lay practitioner inclusion to that of a formal monastic center. Nevertheless, Dogen moved first to Kippoji Temple to be close to the new temple while it was built. The new temple would become Eiheiji, Eternal Peace Temple. During that interlude, Dogen wrote another twenty-nine chapters of *Shobogenzo*, while adjusting to the northern climate of deep snowy winter. In 1246, the first *ango*, a focused, intense practice period, was offered at Eiheiji, establishing Dogen and his followers in the tall pine tree mountains away from the calamitous exchanges of power of the imperial class and established Buddhism.

Now Dogen was faced with the work of organizing daily monastic life and bringing his monks into mature discipline and practice. He turned his focus to rules of behavior for his senior monks as well as care for his junior monks. Dogen's earlier realization concerning the care of food, how to eat, and food preparation were further brought into heightened practice. Each activity of the monks was elevated in a spiritual direction toward the expression of Buddha Nature and the totality of the religious life. The care of the body, clothing, personal conduct, care in eating, were essential to the demonstration of practice as pure Awakening. Because the entire community was living in the establishment and perfect monastic expression of "Eternal Peace," the groundwork of harmony was central to the order and functioning of daily life founded in the practice of Zazen.

Another large body of Dogen's teachings occurs during the latter part of his life. This work, the *Eihei Koroku*, Dogen's Extensive Record, compiles his short, and longer informal talks to his monks, verses of appreciation, commentaries on koans, and poetry. This work further reveals Dogen's poetic versatility and grace in Dharma, which he allowed to flow from him in dynamic generosity and without hesitation throughout his life. After Dogen's death, Koun Ejo would discover, among

Dogen's belongings, his journal writings while in China. Here Dogen had recorded his teacher Rujing's instructions to him from the time they first met until Dogen left China to return to Japan. This work was untitled by Dogen but would be given the title *Hokyo-ki,* or the Record of the Pao-ch'ing Era.

Dogen continued to teach and write, however around the year 1250 his health began to deteriorate and his activities were curtailed. He was advised to go to a warmer climate, but he felt reluctant to leave the sacred ground of Eiheiji. In January 1253, he composed the final chapter of *Shobogenzo,* "Hachi-dainingaku" "On the Eight Realizations of a Great One." He had intended to complete *Shobogenzo* with one hundred chapters, but he would write only ninety-six. At last in summer he was persuaded to leave and seek care in Kyoto. Before departure from Eiheiji, he appointed Koun Ejo, his most excellent and devoted disciple, his successor.

The journey to Kyoto must have been extremely difficult in those days for one in such fragile condition. With Ejo and several other monks alongside, they made their way to the home of a lay disciple, Kakunen, in Kyoto. Dogen's condition had progressed beyond effective treatment. On August 20, 1253, Dogen died in the company of his disciples.

A Note on Style and Formatting

Given the proliferation of Chinese and Japanese words and names that appear in various editions and translations of *Shobogenzo*, and other of Dogen's writings, there is great variety of formatting and usage from one edition to the next. This makes it difficult for an editor to establish a standard when a mix of translations and editions are adopted. Such is the case in this collection of writings. For instance, in one edition of *Shobogenzo*, some words may appear as a hyphenated string of words, yet in another edition appear as one word or as a compound noun. Some of this is due to Dogen's linguistic intention to take us outside of our comfort zone and throw us into a new way of seeing and the translator's way of hearing Dogen. In such a case, the translator will use the means of language in an unconventional way to try to reveal Dogen's linguistic insight and his playfulness with words. Also, a translator may decide to capitalize certain words to arrive at emphasis or heightened meaning in English. Another translator will use lower case. Yet another translator will decide to go back and forth, attempting to bring Dogen's intention to light.

In this collection, the contributors were free to choose their preferred translation of *Shobogenzo*, and their selections can be found in Endnotes immediately following each essay. The formatting of the particular edition and translator is honored. Allowing varied formatting seemed the wisest decision since capitalization or non-capitalization, hyphenated or non-hyphened words may change the intended emphasis that either Dogen or an author is trying to clarify. There was also a decision to not use diacritical marks for the various names and references. There was reasonable effort to use the same basic citation style throughout the essays. These essays, although true to the different translations, intend to provide teaching and commentary on Dogen's thought and Dharma, and to deepen an appreciation of Dogen's wise spiritual prescriptions. Each author is responsible for the content of her essay and for the veracity of the citations. The essays appear in the same order as the fascicles in *Shobogenzo*.

DANCING THE DHARMA

BENDOWA

Teijo Munnich

From the first time I was asked to give a dharma talk by my teacher, Dainin Katagiri Roshi (1928-1990), I felt that the best way to communicate the dharma was simply to do zazen, sitting meditation, and not say a word. I've never actually been brave enough to do this, but when I discovered a story about a Chinese abbot named Yaoshan, I smiled. Here's how it goes: When Yaoshan had not given a dharma talk for a long time, his students approached him and asked him to please come to the dharma hall and give a talk. So he agreed, and went to the lecture hall and took his seat with everyone eagerly awaiting his words of wisdom. But instead of giving a talk, he simply sat quietly for awhile, then got up and left without saying a word. Disappointed, one of his students went to him and asked why he hadn't said anything. His response was that there were scholars for teaching, and he was simply a monk (1).

After returning from my practice at Hosshinji Monastery in 1988, Katagiri Roshi became very ill, so I stayed at the Katagiris' apartment for about a month while he and his wife, Tomoe-san, were at the hospital. When asked to give a lecture, I borrowed Roshi's copy of *Shoyoroku, The Book of Serenity,* to study the story of Yaoshan, and at the end of the story I found a note written by Roshi in Japanese. It said, "There is a way to expound *jijuyu zanmai* with *jijuyu zanmai.*" At the time I had no idea what Roshi meant by this.

The phrase *jijuyu zanmai* comes from a writing called *Bendowa* by Eihei Dogen Zenji written soon after he returned from China (2). After having the note translated, thinking I might gain some insight into the story of Yaoshan, I went back to *Bendowa* to look again at Dogen's description of *jijuyu zanmai.* This is how I became truly interested in the writing of Dogen, and I began by looking more deeply into *Bendowa.*

Bendowa

Katagiri Roshi told us *Bendo* means to carry out the way or to accomplish the way. He said, "The Way is the path through which not only human beings but also all animate and inanimate beings can walk in peace and harmony together... in other words the Way is the absolute truth. The absolute truth is the path" (3).

Wa means "a talk" or "a story." Shohaku Okumura Roshi translates the title "*Bendowa*" as "a talk or discourse about how to practice the Way wholeheartedly" (4).

The subject of the *Bendowa* is *jijuyu zanmai. Jijuyu zanmai* is literally "Samadhi of Self receiving or accepting its function," or "Samadhi of self-enjoyment" or "self-fulfillment." *Ji* is "self"; *ju* is "receive" or "accept"; *yu* is "function" or "use"; *juyu* as a common compound means "fulfillment or enjoyment"; *zanmai* is "Samadhi," usually translated as "concentration" or "one-pointedness" (5).

Why Dogen wrote Bendowa

In the introductory words of *Bendowa*, before describing *jijuyu zanmai*, Dogen Zenji mentions why he is writing *Bendowa*. Finding his teacher, Tendo Nyojo (1163-1228, Tiantong Rujing in Chinese) and his subsequent awakening was a turning point for Dogen; consequently, he felt compelled to help other seekers.

> ... I went to Song [dynasty] China and visited various masters in Zhejiang Province, where I learned the ways of the five schools of Zen. Finally, I met Zen Master Nyojo on Mt Taipai and completely clarified the great matter of life-long practice. After that, I returned home in the first year of Sheting (Shotei, Japanese) (1227). To spread this dharma and to free living beings became my vow. I felt like a heavy burden had been placed on my shoulders.
> In spite of that, I set aside my vow to propagate this, in order to wait for conditions under which it could flourish. For now I will live alone, moving from place to place like a cloud or duckweed, and follow the way of the ancient sages. (6)

The responsibility to help others experience the insights he had experienced weighed heavily on Dogen. I, too, have been affected in profound ways by my teachers and experiences in zazen practice, so I can relate to Dogen's words. I believe a "teacher" is someone who wants to share a deep experience with others who have a sincere wish to pursue the same path. But the dharma is subtle and ungraspable, so teaching seems like an impossible task, and naturally there is some reluctance. Recently someone suggested that feeling a reluctance to teach meant I wasn't being genuine. But for me it is natural to want to share something of great value, even though it is difficult and sometimes feels like a burden. And the sharing keeps taking me back to the essence of this practice. When it came to teaching, even Shakyamuni Buddha is said to have had some hesitation about whether he could show others his experience of awakening. It wasn't because his experience wasn't genuine or that he wanted to keep it to himself, but it's a formidable task to communicate something that is intangible. Clearly Dogen Zenji felt the need to make the effort, but he apparently also realized the difficulty of communicating the dharma.

Dogen also recognized that it wasn't the right moment for him to teach (probably based on the circumstances of his life at that time). Instead, he chose to write about the Way of practice, just in case a future opportunity did not unfold. This is why he chose to write *Bendowa*:

> ... *there might be some sincere practitioners who on their own do not seek after fame or profit and who give priority to the mind that seeks the Way. But they still may be vainly led astray by false teachers, and recklessly cover up correct understanding and become drunk in their own confusion, sinking into delusion for a long time. How will it be possible for [these sincere practitioners] to nurture the true seed of prajna (ultimate wisdom) and have appropriate occasion to attain the Way? Since this unworthy wayfarer (Dogen) is now living like a cloud or duckweed, how will they find the mountain or river where they can visit me? Because I care about these people, I have recollected and written about what I experienced with my own eyes of the style of practice in the Zen monasteries of Song China, and what I received and uphold as the profound teaching of my master. I leave this for devoted practitioners of the way of serenity in order*

to let them know about the true dharma of buddhas. Here is the genuine expression of the essence. (7)

Dogen seems to have been chomping at the bit, trying to figure out how to teach others about the freedom he had found through zazen. At the end of this writing he reiterates his earlier words:

...the essential meaning of engaging the way of zazen has not yet been transmitted in this country, so people who aspire to know it must be sorrowful. For this reason, I have compiled some of what I saw and heard in foreign lands, and have written and preserved my brilliant teacher's true essence in order to make it heard by aspiring practitioners.... (8)

Bendowa was the second of a large body of writings, and in each, Dogen explains some aspect of "the essential meaning of engaging the way of zazen." *Jijuyu zanmai* is the heart of *Bendowa.*_

Jijuyu Zanmai

Dogen begins his discussion of *jijuyu zanmai* with this sentence:

For all ancestors and buddhas who have been dwelling in and maintaining Buddha-dharma, practicing upright sitting in jijuyu zanmai is the true path for opening up enlightenment. (9)

Dogen says that "upright sitting in *jijuyu zanmai*" is the path for "opening up" enlightenment, or awakening. What is translated as "upright sitting" refers to zazen. And he goes on to describe the experience zazen elicits, which he calls *jijuyu zanmai*. *Jijuyu zanmai* could be understood to mean the experience of receiving and using the joy of Samadhi. So what is Samadhi?

Samadhi *(zanmai* in Japanese) is usually translated as "concentration." But this word can be misleading. Concentration is often understood as something we do with our minds; in this case thinking we can use our minds as the primary source of awakening. This is the opposite of what Dogen is trying express.

My first experience of the joy of Samadhi was through dance. Before I met Katagiri Roshi and began to throw myself into zazen practice, I was studying dance and had experienced the letting go that comes when one completely gives oneself over to the form and to the teacher. In order to perform a dance, one has to first learn the steps. After the steps are somewhat mastered, the flow of the dance begins to emerge. At this point resistance arises—one doesn't yet have a total picture of the dance, but through the steps and the flow there is a sense of accomplishment, which seems to be enough. Then weariness sets in and there doesn't seem to be anything else to do, maybe there is a feeling that going further is beyond the ability of the dancer. So the next part of the process is to continue dancing, to go beyond that resistance and exhaust it. At that point, the dancer becomes the dance and is danced. There is no longer any effort. And the dance is perfect.

Although my experience of Samadhi through dance was wondrous, at the time I didn't recognize the process and didn't even see it as a process. I simply saw it as something that happened sometimes when I danced. One of the benefits of studying with a teacher is that by trusting and submitting to the teacher's guidance, letting go happens. To follow an aspiration is an important component, but if we do it alone, we have only our own experiences to draw from, and because our experiences are limited, it's easy to go in circles. We look at and judge what we're doing, seeing it only from one perspective, our own. But a teacher allows us to enter into the process in ways we haven't imagined and then nudges us to continue just when we think we can't go on. A teacher can help to get beyond resistance.

Samadhi is the kind of concentration in which you absolutely merge; there is no distinction between you and what you are doing. Sometimes Samadhi is translated as "one-pointedness." This means the ability to stay in touch with and return to the source of awakening. The source of awakening is reality itself, simply described as impermanence and no-self. Impermanence is the movement of life, the changing, exchanging, and re-arranging that everything in life is doing in every moment. It is simultaneously death and birth, moment by moment. No-self describes our relationship with life. There is not a definable self that exists separate from everything else in life. What we call "myself" is part of, and dependent on, the life of all things. And this is true of everything. So when one thing changes, everything changes. The movement is constant. This is what we awaken to when we let go of our ideas about life. Dogen talks about it in this way:

When one displays the Buddha mudra with one's whole body and mind, sitting upright in this Samadhi even for a short time, everything in the entire dharma world becomes Buddha mudra, and all space in the universe completely becomes enlightenment. Therefore, it enables Buddha-tathagatas to increase the dharma joy of their own original grounds and renew the adornment of the way of awakening. Simultaneously, all living beings of the dharma world in the ten directions and six realms become clear and pure in body and mind, realize great emancipation, and their own original face appears. At that time, all things together awaken to supreme enlightenment and utilize Buddha-body.... (10)

and

There is a path through which the anunttara samyak sam-bodi (incomparable awareness) of all things returns [to the person in zazen], and whereby [that person and the enlight-enment of all things] intimately and imperceptibly assist each other. Therefore this zazen person without fail drops off body and mind, cuts away previous tainted views and thoughts, awakens genuine Buddha-dharma, universally helps the Buddha work in each place, as numerous as atoms, where Buddha-tathagatas teach and practice, and widely influ-ences practitioners who are going beyond buddha, vigorously exalting the dharma which goes beyond Buddha. (11)

In order to awaken to the truth of life or reality, we first have to become free of our self-imposed restrictions, the delusions which cause us to adhere to the belief that there is something to depend on that is lasting and that our life is in some way unique. Recognizing impermanence, we are aware of the infinite possibilities that are always present in life, rather than being stuck in our perceptions of what is possible. Being aware of interconnectedness, we naturally experience the support of everything in life. This is what we awaken to and return to in zazen. And this is called *jijuyu zanmai.*

Life is everything and everything is life. We are part of the ten-direction-dharma-realm and are not separate from anything. Everything in life is dependent on every-thing else. *Jijuyu zanmai* is the experience, dancing and being danced by life.

When Dogen Zenji describes *jijuyu zanmai,* he in-cludes everything as part of that dance:

At this time, because earth, grasses and trees, fences and walls, tiles and pebbles, all things in the ten-direction-dharma-realm, carry out Buddha work, therefore everyone receives the benefit of wind and water caused by this functioning, and all are imperceptibly helped by the wondrous and incomprehensible influence of Buddha to actualize the enlightenment at hand. (12)

Then he tells us that this isn't something we can recognize with our conscious minds.

However, these various [mutual influences] do not mix into the perceptions of the person sitting, because they take place within stillness without any fabrication and they are enlightenment itself. If practice and enlightenment were separate, as people commonly believe, it would be possible for them to perceive each other. But that which is associated with perceptions cannot be the standard of enlightenment because deluded human sentiment cannot reach the standard of enlightenment. (13)

Perceiving *jijuyu zanmai* is defining enlightenment. Believing that our fabrication of enlightenment is the experience itself is not the same as being one with it. Before the dance the dancer imagines the dance, and after the dance becomes a spectator. *Jijuyu zanmai* is being within the experience of dance, the experience of life. *Jijuyu zanmai* is the complete dance of life in each moment. How can we do this? It is not the usual way we accomplish something. Dogen speaks of "disporting oneself freely" as the way of zazen.

Disporting with the buddhas

For disporting oneself freely in this Samadhi, practicing zazen in upright posture is the true gate. (14)

When I first encountered the word "disporting" while reading *Bendowa*, I thought that I was misunderstanding something in the nuance of the translation, because disporting means "to amuse oneself." When I checked the characters for disporting – *yuge* – in my Japanese-English dictionary, I discovered that *yu* means "to play; enjoy oneself"; and *ge* means "to play or frolic." That both of these characters meant to play was at first surprising to me—I had always thought of Dogen Zenji as a very serious person. So I was happy to discover this description of *jijuyu zanmai* in *Bendowa*.

In a lecture given by Katagiri Roshi about yuge he said: "*Yu* is 'to play': ge: means 'to transform.' So *yuge* means you can transform yourself in the process of playing freely. Transform does not mean change. Without changing your body and mind, capability and ability, your habits, your heredity, your karma, something transforms in the process of playing freely."

There is a transformation that takes place when we play freely. As children, most of us could and did experience this. But this freedom is harder to access as adults. In the process of learning how to survive in the world, we develop an adherence to reality only in its functional sense and lose touch with its absolute nature. This is why Dogen Zenji teaches us about *jijuyu zanmai* and tells us it means to play freely in this Samadhi. Our practice of zazen should be the same. Dogen taught the practice of *shikantaza*, of "just sitting" without grasping, without techniques or methods. Just sitting allows us to experience things as they are in each moment. All we have to do is drop our compulsion to want to do something. Then we can see the bigger picture of reality beyond what we are able to define or understand intellectually.

Letting the dance unfold

When you let go, the dharma fills your hands; it is not within the boundary of one or many. (15)

The Samadhi I experienced through dance was based on specific choreographic forms. Dogen's choreography for *jijuyu zanmai* is based on one simple form - upright sitting – and within this form the dance of life unfolds. In dance this is called improvisation. Letting life unfold means to awaken to life in each moment. Within the posture, within quiet sitting, there is continuous, but imperceptible, movement – our blood continues to circulate, our breathing continues, our heart keeps beating... the spirit of free play becomes stronger as our bodies settle into the posture. It may seem counter-intuitive to say that in stillness we experience the dance, but there is always movement within stillness and stillness within movement. This is life.

To let go is to open our hands. Standing with hands open is standing with our minds open. Sitting quietly, without doing anything, we open our hands and receive life as it is. This is *jijuyu zanmai*. Letting go means to "let it be."

In *Fukanzazengi* Dogen gives instructions about how to let go. "Do not interfere with the workings of the mind, nor try to control the movements of your thoughts" (16). Dogen says very simply "do not interfere." Let it be. He elaborates by saying: "Think of not thinking. How is this done? By leaving thinking as-it-is.

This is the essential method of zazen" (17). The art of Dogen's zazen is to simply let ourselves be absorbed into the moment, to play with life. When we do not impose our perceptions, our visions about the outcome, we enter into the dance of life.

I once asked Katagiri Roshi, if Samadhi could be experienced through art forms such as dance or through sports or other activities, why was it necessary to do zazen. He said that when we experience it through a specific activity, we might think that the experience is unique to that activity. But awakening is not confined to any one thing – everything we do is an opportunity for awakening. Life itself is the source of *jijuyu zanmai*. Zazen helps us to see how to find the joy of awakening in all aspects of life.

"There is a way to expound jijuyu zanmai with jijuyu zanmai."

The wholehearted practice of the Way...allows all things to exist in enlightenment, and enables us to live out oneness in the path of emancipation. When we break through the barrier and drop off all limitations, we are no longer concerned with conceptual distinctions. (18)

One time at the beginning of a talk I sat quietly for a period of time. The tension in the air was palpable. I recalled someone who had sat like this once when he was supposed to give a short student talk during a Practice Period. Though I suspected he was trying to do what Yaoshan did, and I respected him for that, I found myself judging him as arrogant, and maybe even a bit lazy. So when I sat quietly and felt the tension as everyone waited for me to say something, I imagined that I was being judged and I judged myself. Who did I think I was?

Yaoshan had to have had great confidence in zazen practice to sit quietly as he did, and then to get up without saying one word. Clearly he understood that the best way to express the truth of what we awaken to in zazen was through his complete and wholehearted embodiment of zazen.

Endnotes

(1) *Book of Serenity*, Trans. Thomas Cleary. Hudson, NY: Lindesfarne Press, 1990. Case #7, 28.

(2) Eihei Dogen. *The Wholehearted Way, Bendowa*. Trans. Shohaku Okumura and Taigen Daniel Leighton. Boston: Tuttle, 1997.

(3) Lecture given by Dainin Katagiri, September 20, 1977.

(4) Okumura & Leighton, 10.

(5) Ibid., 43.

(6) Ibid., 20.

(7) Ibid.

(8) Ibid., 41

(9) Ibid., 21.

(10) Ibid., 22.

(11) Ibid.

(12) Ibid.

(13) Ibid.

(14) Ibid., 19

(15) Ibid.

(16) Eihei Dogen. *Fukan-Zazengi*. In: Harada, Sekkei. *The Essence of Zen*. Trans. Ed. Daigaku Rumme. Tokyo: Kodansha, 1998. 138.

(17) Ibid., 144.

(18) Okumura and Leighton, 19.

ONE BRIGHT JEWEL

Ikka no Myoju

Shotai De La Rosa

I would like to express my deep gratitude to my teacher Shohaku Okumura Roshi. Without his devotion to the practice and teachings of Dogen Zenji I would not have been able to study the teachings of the great Japanese Zen Master. I do not know the Japanese language and through the many Genzo-e, teaching retreats, with Okumura Roshi I had the opportunity to get closer to the perception of Dogen Zenji. This, coupled with the intense practice of zazen, has been and still is of invaluable support in my life. Finally, my profound respect and gratitude to Eihei Dogen that is opening up something that still I cannot understand. I am working on the Spanish translation of his extensive records and I feel that he is revealing himself more and more through his strong and authentic way of expressing Buddha Dharma.

Instead of the most used English title, "*One Bright Pearl*," I choose One Bright Jewel (1). Dogen is expressing his insight of the reality of all beings that "it is perfect roundness, and roundly it rolls along" and "Its colors and light, as they are, are endless" (2). These images and others he makes use of, made me think that Dogen is talking about a gem that is bright and has no color, and for the fact of having no color, the gem manifests all the infinite colors. A pearl has color, generally white. The image of a jewel recalls something clear that, as a jewel on a knot of Indra's net, it simultaneously reflects all others and is reflected in each one. Also, in his English translation of Eto Sokuo book, *Zen Master Dogen as Founding Patriarch,* Ichimura Shohei translated this fascicle as "One Bright Jewel" (3).

After leaving behind his life as a fisherman, Gensha Shibi (835-908) was ordained as a Vinaya monk. Later, he went to Mt. Seppo to study with Seppo Gison (822-908). He was well known for his ascetic practice.

In a time where it was common to travel to study with several teachers, Dogen points out that Shibi studied only with one, Seppo, and although being a fisherman without any knowledge of sutras and commentaries, he has a "deep aspiration to study the way." Here we see two important aspects of Dogen's teachings: first, it is useless to travel around if we have already found a true teacher under whom we are studying exhaustively. "We do not esteem idly entering one monastery and leaving another monastery as thorough exploration. We esteem discovery with the whole of the eyes as thorough exploration. We esteem attainment of the ultimate through action as thorough exploration. To see, through the end, how thick is the skin of the face: this is thorough exploration" (4). Second, arousing bodhicitta is fundamental for the practice of the way. "The Ancestoral (sic)

Master Nagarjuna said that the mind that solely sees the impermanence of this world of constant appearance and disappearance is called bodhi-mind. Therefore, [for now I think it would be appropriate to talk about] bodhi-mind as the mind that sees impermanence" (5). And, "In my formal speeches or lectures too, I emphasize that impermanence is swift; life-and-death is the great matter. Reflect on this reality again and again in your heart without forgetting it, and without wasting a moment. Put your whole mind into the practice of the Way. Remember that you are alive only today in this moment" (6).

In this fascicle, Dogen examines thoroughly a dialogue between Gensha Shibi and a monk. The dialogue is: "I have heard the Master's words that the whole Universe in ten directions is one bright pearl." "How should the student understand [this]?" Gensha says, "The whole Universe in ten directions is one bright pearl." "What use is understanding?" Another day Gensha asks the monk, "The whole Universe in ten directions is one bright pearl." "How do you understand [this]?" The monk says, "The whole universe in ten directions is one bright pearl." "What use is understanding?" Gensha answers, I see that you are struggling to get inside a demon's cave in a black mountain" (7).

With his profound insight, Dogen analyzes the koan word by word. For him Shibi's utterance is about the reality of all beings, the Bright Jewel that is boundless, does not belong to the world of dualism, does not have a feature and it is not unmanifested. However, for Dogen, non-dualism is essentially inseparable from dualism, not its opposite, otherwise the non-duality will be dualistic. Likewise, by not having a feature and flowing endlessly, the Bright Jewel can take any feature according with the circumstances, while, simultaneously, it is sweeping alone without stopping even for an instant. That is, impermanence never stops and has no feature, but it is always manifesting in accordance with different conditions. Furthermore, because it is "not in a state of vigorous activity, and not disclosed in perfect clarity," although not concealed, it is not evident. Dogen is not comparing or making distinctions of what is or what is not the Bright Jewel, because the Bright Jewel *is* the ten directions of the whole universe and not something that is *in* the ten directions. There is not something called "ten directions" in something called "the whole universe." Overall, there is not "something" named "Bright Jewel."

"Moreover, because it is not birth-and-death, and it is not coming and going, it is birth-and-death and coming and going. This being so, it is the past gone from here; it is the present come from here" (8).

Our lives are birth-and-death, coming and going; a moment by moment relationship between us, the subjects, and all the conditions we encounter, the objects. Still, is a relationship subject-object void of any fixed, established substance, whether we call it subject or object. Therefore, Dogen says, the Bright Jewel is birth and death, coming and going. It is in the midst of our daily lives that the Bright Jewel manifests itself. The Bright Jewel is the Bright Jewel manifesting the Bright Jewel each moment in a time that has no beginning or end, and in a space that is boundless. Apart from the phenomenal world, the ten directions, there is not a future Bright Jewel to attain. Realizing the emptiness of the phenomenal world, within the phenomenal world, is how the Bright Jewel reveals itself. If we attach ourselves to the objects we encounter, meaning, if we live pulled *only* by our discriminating mind, the Bright Jewel will not manifest, although the attachment is also the working of the Bright Jewel. The ten-directions-phenomenal-world, is just a web of causes and conditions moving with no end in an infinite time and space, inter and intra weaving everything without obstruction. Yet, this "everything" and the weaving is not other than the Bright Jewel unfolding itself right now and right here, beyond the dichotomy of particularity and wholeness, but keeping the distinctiveness of each one aspect.

There are not good-bad, like-dislike extremes in the Bright Jewel. It does not have form, feeling, perception, volition or consciousness, yet it manifests itself as form, feeling, and so on. In his unique interpretation of this dialogue, Dogen does not identify with the conventional interpretation, that Gensha is the enlightened teacher that is testing the student understanding, while the monk is snared on his intellect.

Continuing with Nishijima and Cross translation, *"The whole of the ten directions* describes the ceaseless [process] of pursuing things to make them into self, and of pursuing self to make it into something. The arising of emotion and the distinctions of the intellect, which we describe as separation, are themselves [as real as] turning the head and changing the face, or developing things and throwing [oneself] into the moment. Because we pursue self to make it into something, the whole of the ten directions is in the ceaseless state. And because [the whole of the ten directions] is a fact before the moment, it sometimes overflows beyond [our] regulating ability which is the pivot of the moment" (9).

Dogen describes the whole ten directions as the unfolding interaction of self and others, which are the web of cause and conditions, the phenomenal world working freely. In the phenomenal world-bright-jewel, if an emotion arises whether we run after it or reject it, neither wisdom nor separation hinders each other. For Dogen, wisdom, non-discrimination and separation, discrimination-karmic consciousness, are both a function of the Bright Jewel. The reality of all beings, the ten directions of the whole universe, is always disclosing itself. This does not mean that we can do whatever we want or that we do not need to practice because we live in the reality of all beings that is wisdom. It is all the way around. The reality of all beings, the Bright Jewel, is not our possession, and our practice is endless. This is the way that enlightenment-bright-jewel unfolds and is not because of our individual effort, but if we do not take care of our practice diligently, we will not be able to "see" the Bright Jewel: an on going practice beyond enlightenment. That is our practice. Therefore, what we call "separation" is itself "[as real as] turning the head and changing the face, or developing things and throwing [oneself] into the moment" (10). If we shift perspectives, we will be able to meet with the infinite expressions of the reality. Wisdom, the master flinging the reality, and illusion, the monk bringing about his understanding, are two aspects of the Bright Jewel itself. Nevertheless, seeing whatever we encounter as an object or as the reality, does not mean that we will be able to control the functioning of the same reality. Although the interaction between self and others does not stop even for an instant, the ten directions of the whole universe "is ungraspable even in the essence of the activity," "because its own nature is prior to such activity" (11).

Next, Dogen expresses his insight about time and space. *"The one bright pearl* goes directly through the thousand years: the eternal past has not ended, but the eternal present has arrived. The body exists now, and the mind exists now. Even so, [the whole Universe] is a bright pearl. It is not grass and trees there and here, it is not mountains and rivers at all points of the compass; it is a bright pearl" (12).

Dogen's vision of time is deeply connected with his teaching on Buddha-nature.

Because the lack of space and because it is not the aim of this commentary, I am not going into the complexity of *Bussho* (The Buddha-nature) and *Uji* (Being-Time), but would like to mention three prominent points regarding Dogen's teachings on time and Buddha-nature. First, his consideration about the present moment that does not move. Dogen emphasizes that there is only one way to measure time and it is in the present moment. Nevertheless, the present moment does not move because it is empty; it is not that there are different present moments that happened in the present. Each moment of time is independent and it is time in its fullest. "So the present moment has no length, a length of zero. This is to say, the present moment is *empty*" (13).

Second, Dogen talks about the inseparability of the unmovable-present-moment, and ourselves. "Time and being are identified with each other" (14). Thus, there is not time that is not us and we are time, being-time. Third, Dogen rejected the notion of a potential Buddha-nature and affirms the non fixed Buddha-nature on the grounds of impermanence. Buddha-nature is not a seed waiting to manifest through practice. Buddha-nature is itself, impermanence.

Dogen does not negate our perception of time as flowing from the past to the future, but what he stresses is that each and every moment is independent and not a continuity of fractions. The no continuity of each and every moment has its roots, precisely, in impermanence, the simultaneity of appearance-disappearance of the phenomenal world that makes each time a complete time and Buddha-nature a complete space. In short, now and here is "the bottomless present moment, in which, according to Buddhism, the circularity of past and future are contained" (15), the time of each and everything in the whole universe. Hence the body exists now and the mind exists now, in a time that does not flow, the time of the Bright-Jewel-impermanence-Buddha-nature. What we call grass or tree or mountains or rivers are the Bright Jewel manifesting the fullness of time and space.

"How can I gain understanding of that? This utterance makes it seem as though the monk's karmic consciousness is at play, yet it is the manifestation of the great function which is the great law" (16). With his unconventional interpretation Dogen views the monk's words as an utterance and not as a question. Notwithstanding, he does not negate that the monk is expressing his intellectual understanding, Dogen's own position has a unique feature, and he declares firmly that the monk's utterance is likewise the Bright Jewel manifesting as the great function, the reality of all beings "which is the Great Standard itself"(17) or the great law as translated by Waddell and Abe. And this great standard or great law is the law of cause and effect, which is grounded on moral conduct. We are free to live either based on discrimination or going beyond discrimination, both are the unfolding of the Bright Jewel, but the consequences are different.

"Progressing further, we should make it strikingly obvious that a foot of water is a one foot wave: in other words, a yard of the pearl is a yard of brightness" (18). Wave and water are not two separate things; there is not a wave without water. Waves are illusions on the surface of the serene water of enlightenment; both are the Bright Jewel manifesting as brightness. In the great function, the law of cause and effect is thoroughly working with absolute freedom. We need regulations to follow, guidelines of moral conduct that help us to not stick blindly to our karmic consciousness. Together with all beings we are part of the great function, which does not matter if we realize it or not, but we need to make our best effort, moment by moment, to awaken to that reality. That is our practice with no end. Dogen's zazen, *shikantaza,* is sitting on the ground of the great function.

Then, Dogen says that Gensha's words, *"The whole Universe in ten directions is one bright pearl. What use is understanding?"* are expressions of the truth of the dharma that Buddha inherits from Buddha, ancestor from ancestor, and Gensha from Gensha. He continues saying that it is a transmission that cannot be avoided, but even if a Buddha or an ancestor or Gensha "did clearly escape it for a while, the very fact of their utterance is the unmitigated occasion of the Bright Pearl's manifestation" (19). The role of language in Dogen occupies a prominent place in his teaching career. He does not identify himself with the common Zen teaching that the intellect is useless, that silence prevails upon words, that it is not possible to talk about the reality, and the like. Language operates in the realm of discrimination, but that is also how the Bright Jewel expresses itself. To awaken to the reality is not enough; we must express it with words and actions. For Dogen, Gensha is uttering the truth of the Dharma; he is using language to expound the reality to the monk. According with the conventional interpretation of "What use is understanding?" what Gensha is saying to the monk is: "It is worthless to use your intellect, stop thinking." But for Dogen, Gensha's utterance is in itself the truth transmitted from Buddha to Buddha, from ancestor to ancestor, and from Gensha to Gensha, and the transmission is the function of the Bright Jewel. In other words, the transmission from the Bright Jewel to the Bright Jewel manifesting itself in the phenomenal world is the whole universe in the ten directions. Gensha may try to escape from the transmission saying, "Stop thinking" or "The understanding is useless," but his own ability to express the Dharma declaring, "The whole universe in ten directions is one Bright Pearl," is the Bright Jewel unwrapping itself freely (20).

The next day, Gensha asks the monk what is his understanding of "the whole universe is One Bright Pearl." Dogen reads this dialogue as interplay between two levels of approaching the truth. Gensha is shifting his mode of showing the reality, from "stop thinking, it is useless" to "inquire, think." The monk answers, "The whole universe in ten directions is One Bright Pearl. What use is understanding?" is "mounting the robber's horse to chase the robber" (21). Playing back, the monk makes use of Gensha's utterance and utters his own comprehension: my understanding is that understanding is not useless, but at the same time it is never sufficient for penetrating the truth. And Dogen alerts the monk saying, "It is a matter of practicing within a creature different from himself" (22). "A creature different from himself" or "going among alien beings" (23) is Dogen teaching about practicing within the world of polarities, going beyond them. In other words, the practice does not discriminate between sameness and difference, but embraces both simultaneously. The practice of, "just turn your light inward and reflect, how many 'What is there to understand?' can there be" (24)?

In *Fukanzazengi*, Dogen instructs, "You should therefore cease from practice based on intellectual understanding, pursuing words and following after speech, and learn the backward step that turns your light inward to illuminate your self. Body and mind will drop away from themselves, and your original face will manifest itself. If you wish to attain suchness, you should practice suchness without delay" (25). Dogen is giving instructions about zazen and here he is saying that to sit zazen we should leave aside our discriminating mind and allow the self to show its true nature, and the self Dogen is speaking of is the self that is forgotten when it is verified by all things. In this verification "the body and mind of the self and the body and mind of others drop off" (26). So, turning the light inward to illuminate the self is the practice of zazen. When we sit we let go of our thoughts; we do not follow or reject them; they come and go without our doing anything to control them. That is how the body and mind of the self and others, discrimination, separation, drop off, and that happens, not because of our will power or our understanding.

How many teachings of "what is there to understand" can there be in the practice of "turning the light inward"? Dogen affirms, "I might say, "seven pieces of cheese." I might say "five bean cakes" (27). When the self is illuminated and the body and mind of the self and others drop off, it is futile trying to make evaluations with our thinking mind. Still, in our daily lives we have to make decisions according to different circumstances. In order to do so, we have to think, to ascertain, to investigate. Hence, there are innumerable ways to study and understand the teachings, but at the same time, moment by moment we face concrete occurrences that call for attention and decision making; but when we sit zazen, we abandon our discriminations allowing the self to illuminate. In any manner, it is the Bright Jewel manifesting itself as the gold "South of the [River] Sho and North of the [River] Tan" (28).

After hearing the monk's words, Gensha says, "Now I know that you are living in the Cave of Demons on Black Mountain" (29). Although this sounds as if Gensha is

undermining the monk's presentation of his understanding as coming from his karmic consciousness, and
probably this is Gensha's intention, Dogen clarifies its
significance equally to the function of the Bright Jewel.
In a similar vein, he states, "Be aware that from antiquity
the face of the sun and the face of the moon have never changed" (30). This statement from Dogen appears
contradictory with his emphasis on impermanence, but
looking closely we can see that his aim is to show that the
continuous activity of the Bright Jewel is emptiness, the
true nature of the ten directions of the entire universe.
Moreover, saying 'face of the sun' we are referring to
the sun; saying 'face of the moon' we make mention
of the moon. So, the face of the sun is not the face of
the moon, and the face of the moon is not the face of
the sun. Both, sun and moon are independent partic-
ularities with its own features and characteristics, and
at the same time, they partake of the impermanence
that pervades the universe. There is not an unalterable
thing called 'face of the sun' or 'face of the moon,' they
are empty as everything everywhere in the timeless time
and in the space-less space. There is not a single thing
that is not susceptible to the transiency. Hence, "each
moment everything is new and fresh" (31), right here,
right now. On that basis, Dogen's approach highlights
his view that there is no objective reality aside from the
emptiness of the entire universe. And, "if I say in the six
month [my name is] 'Right Now', that does not mean
my name is "Hot" (32). In emptiness, "right now" is the
real face of each and everything and the distinctiveness
is only transitional features in the everlasting scenery of
impermanence-bright-jewel.

Dogen goes on explaining the real reality of the Bright
Jewel, its beginningless beginning, and, a key aspect of
Dogen's insight, the wholeness of the Bright Jewel itself.

There is one Bright Jewel, not two, not three, he says. By no means, he is declaring firmly that there is one reality, that is, the conditioned reality of the entire universe in ten directions which is empty, being emptiness its true nature. "Without being discussed as two pearls or three pearls, the Whole Body is one right-Dharma-eye, the Whole Body is real substance, the Whole Body is one phrase, the Whole Body is brightness, and the Whole Body is the Whole Body itself" (33). The conditioned world is the reality and my entire body itself is the true Dharma eye, meaning wisdom; my entire body is the true form of the body of Buddha; my entire body is the unique expression "the whole universe in ten directions is one bright pearl"; my entire body is the brightness of the self in the whole universe in ten directions (34); my entire body is my entire body itself. Consequently, my entire body does not obstruct my entire body. The true nature of my entire body is emptiness. Emptiness does not hinder emptiness. Emptiness is the round seamless whole turning over and over, and over with total freedom.

"Since the pearl's merit is manifested in this way, the Bodhisattvas Kannon and Miroku are, here and now, seeing forms and hearing sounds; old Buddhas and new Buddhas are bodily manifested, preaching the Dharma" (35). The Bright Jewel manifests itself in the conditioned world, where there are forms and sounds. If we awaken to the reality of all beings, the real reality of the phenomenal world, penetrating the true nature of sounds and forms moment by moment, we will be able to be with Kannon and Maitreya, and will see and hear all past, present and future Buddhas preaching the Dharma. That is the virtue of the Bright Jewel.

Next, in his unique way of expressing the Dharma and using descriptions and parables from sutras, for

example from the *Lotus Sutra,* Dogen describes different ways the Bright Jewel displays itself, moment by
moment. "Just at the moment of the present, whether
suspended in space or hanging inside a garment, whether kept under a [dragon] chin or kept in a top-knot,
[the one bright pearl] in all cases, is one bright pearl
throughout the whole Universe in ten directions" (36).
Dogen's aim is to show us that the Bright Jewel is always
before our eyes and it is not concealed, does not matter
if sewn in a garment or hanging in the space or beneath
the chin of a dragon or inside an adornment for the
head. All of these are the specific situations in which
the Bright Jewel comes forward, according with causes
and conditions in the vast and timeless web. In addition, he says, "To hang inside a garment is its situation,
so do not say that it will be dangling on the surface. To
hang inside a top one knot or under a chin is its situation, so do not expect to play with it on the surface of
the top-knot or on the surface of the chin" (37).

Dogen is warning us not to try to modify things and
circumstances or situations in a futile attempt to find
something veiled called "bright jewel." The way things
are in this present moment is the distinguishing attribute of each and everyone in the ten directions of the
whole universe. And all the characteristics of a given
moment are the criterion for the Bright Jewel to show
itself plainly; it is not because of our personal effort. Our
practice is to awaken to the changing reality moment after moment. When we sit zazen we sit on the foundation
of the reality. In other words, the whole universe in the
directions sits in the ten directions of the whole universe.

Making use of the parable on the chapter of the
Lotus Sutra, Dogen adds, "When you are drunk, there is
a close friend who will give the pearl to you, and you as
well must without fail impart the pearl to a close friend.

When the pearl is attached to someone, he is invariably drunk. It being thus, it is the one bright pearl-all the universe" (38). The Bright Jewel is always evident, but we are limited individuals who cannot see the wholeness; we are part of the Bright Jewel; attached to it; drunk on it. We can only experience the unfolding of the Bright Jewel when we face the different circumstances in our daily lives, until we awaken to the fact that we and the circumstances are the Bright Jewel, the ten directions in the whole universe, opening and spreading out timelessly with no borders. Consequently, and regardless of the fact that the Bright Jewel does not have *a* face, we will be able to see that it shows itself with an infinite number of faces, changing features, shapes, colors, coming to an end, taking action. And the realization that all of this *is* the Bright Jewel is how we meet with the Bright Jewel, our true nature, our original face. It does not matter if we believe it or not. Our confusion is in thinking that it is of no value to even imagine that we are the Bright Jewel, and not a stable, permanent self, that is, the Bright Jewel presenting itself as of no value. Thus, Dogen says, "although its face seems to keep on changing, turning and stopping, it is the same bright pearl. Knowing that the pearl is indeed like this, that itself is the bright pearl. In this way the colorations and configurations of the bright pearl are encountered. When it is thus, there is no reason to doubtingly think that you are not the pearl because you perplexedly think, 'I am not the pearl.' Perplexing thoughts, doubts, and our accepting or rejecting are but passing, trivial notions. It is, moreover, only the pearl appearing as a trivial notion" (39).

Next, Dogen urges, "How could we not love the bright pearl? Its color and light, as they are, are endless. Each color and every ray of light at each moment and in every situation is the virtue of the whole Universe in ten directions; who would want to plunder it? No one would throw a tile into a street market" (40).

With the awareness of the multiplicity and variety of circumstances we encounter, it is impossible to not love the infinite colors and radiance that the totality of the phenomenal world offers to us at each moment. It is the merit of the ten directions in the whole universe. There are no useless or priceless things within it. There is nothing to throw away in the entire universe.

Furthermore, Dogen says, "Do not worry about falling or not falling into the six states of cause and effect. They are the original state of being right from head to toe, which is never unclear, and the bright pearl is its features and the bright pearl is its eyes" (41).

Dogen gives us his profound vision about how to live our lives with our whole body and mind with the complete awareness of our unquestionable individuality and that our being, at the same time, is part of the whole of infinite numbers of others unquestionable individualities. Simply, I am I and not you. I am responsible for what I do, think and say. No one can do that for me. And when I sit zazen, I do sit on the ground of the reality of all beings where there is no "I" or "you." Nevertheless, in my day-to-day life, where I have to make distinctions as an individual person, I should manifest my uniqueness within the wholeness I am part of. So, disappearance, being not afraid of falling or not falling, I should not be unwilling to perceive the law of cause and effect (42).

The Bright Jewel is and has been completely clear, keeping its freshness and beauty, even when surrounded by causality. We should not be fearful of transmigrating within the six realms of existence, means we should not be filled with fear of living in samsara, but recognize how to live in samsara awakened to the impermanence of all things, including ourselves, and helping others to attain the same realization.

"Still, neither I nor you know what the bright pearl or what the bright pearl is not. Hundreds of thoughts and hundreds of negations of thought have combined to form a very clear idea. At the same time, by virtue of Gensha's words of Dharma, we have heard, recognized and clarified the situation of a body-and-mind which has already become the bright pearl" (43).

Notwithstanding, the Bright Jewel is not hidden and reveals itself in the innumerable shapes and features, colors, smells and sounds. We do not know what the Bright Jewel is or what is not, generating our own point of views in our effort to hold onto something that meets our needs for permanence. But, at the end, the realization goes forward in addition to include both at the same time.

That is the "very clear idea"; a combination of "hundreds of thoughts and hundreds of negation of thoughts." Simultaneously, the realization that from the beginning our body-mind *is* the Bright Jewel becomes apparent by virtue of Gensha's utterance. "Thereafter, the mind is not personal; why should we be worried by attachment to whether it is a bright pearl or is not a bright pearl, as if what arises and passes were some person. Even surmising and worry is not different from the bright pearl. No action nor any thought has ever been caused by anything other than the bright pearl" (44).

When we realize that our body-mind with all its thoughts, no thoughts, its hearing, smelling, and so on, is itself the Bright Jewel, our notions of "I," "me" and "mine" drop off by the power of the ten directions of the entire universe. Realizing that our real true nature is impersonal, empty of any substance, that appears and disappears, we are not bothered anymore about if we are or not the Bright Jewel. In other words, that there is or there is not the Bright Jewel is not the point, but rather awakening to the impermanence of each and everything in the whole universe in ten directions, including us, is the cause of each thing without exception that has been happening since the beginningless beginning.

"Therefore, forward steps and backward steps in a demon's black-mountain cave are just the one bright pearl itself" (45). Besides our daily life, with its ups and downs, there is nothing else called "Bright Jewel," but in the midst of the always changing reality, we must wholeheartedly decide to live, with the choice to follow blindly our desires, or to cultivate the practice of the Bright Jewel together with all beings.

Endnotes

(1)   I changed the English translation of the title, based on my studies with my teacher Shohaku Okumura Roshi and his lectures on this chapter during a Genzo-e in May 2009 at Sanshin Zen Community in Bloomington. Basically, I used the translation from Nishijima & Cross. Book 1, *Master Dogen's Shobogenzo.* Woods Hole: Windbell Publications, 1994. 39-44, the translation of Norman Waddell & Masao Abe, *The Heart of Dogen's Shobogenzo.* Albany: State University of New York Press, 2002. 31-37, and the working draft translation from my teacher.

(2)   Nishijima and Cross, Book 1, 42-43.

(3)   Ichimura Shohei, trans., *Zen Master Dogen as Founding Patriarch.* Washington: North American Institute of Zen Studies, 2001. 635.

(4)   See Nishijima & Cross, *Master Dogen's Shobogenzo,* Shobogenzo Hensan, Book 3, 207-214

(5)   See *The Heart of Zen, Practice without Gaining-mind,* trans. Shohaku Okumura, Tokyo: Soto-shu Shumucho, 2006. 6-35.

(6)   Shobogenzo Zuimonki 2-14, trans. Shohaku Okumura, Tokyo: Soto-shu Shumucho, , 2004. 93.

(7)   Nishijima and Cross, Book 1, 40.

(8)   Waddell, Norman and Masao Abe, *The Heart of Dogen's Shobogenzo,* Albany: State University of New York Press, 2002. 33.xs.

(9)   Nishijima and Cross, 41.

(10) Ibid.

(11) Waddell and Abe, 34.

(12) Nishijima and Cross, 41.

(13) Shohaku Okumura, *Realizing Genjokoan, The Key to Dogen's Shobogenzo.* Boston: Wisdom Publications, 2010. 118.

(14) Ibid., 119-120.

(15) Heine, Steven, *Dogen and the Koan Tradition, A Tale of Two Shobogenzo Texts.* Albany: State University of New York Press, 1994. 71.

(16) Waddell and Abe, 34.

(17) Nishijima and Cross, Book 1, 41.

(18) Ibid.

(19) Waddell and Abe, 34.

(20) Regarding Dogen's vision of language, I would like to mention the study of Steven Heine about the nature of Japanese and its influence in Dogen. After discussing the interrelationship between language and mind he presented his view that, "Dogen inherited and helped culminate a tradition in which the intimate connection between language and phenomena is sustained by the human capacity to express the true nature of things as they are in both their profound mystery (*yugen*) and utter simplicity." See Steven Heine, *Dogen and the Koan tradition, A Tale of Two Shobogenzo Texts*, Albany: State University of New York Press, 1994. 142-144.

(21) Ibid., 35.

(22) Ibid., 35.

(23) Nishijima and Cross, Book 1, 42.

(24) Waddell and Abe, 35.

(25) Ibid., 3.

(26) Shohaku Okumura, *Realizing Genjokoan, The Key to Dogen's Shobogenzo*, Boston: Wisdom Publications, 2010. 75.

(27) Waddell and Abe, 35.

(28) Ibid., 35, footnote 13 and Nishijima and Cross, Book 1, 42.

(29) Waddell and Abe, 35.

(30) Ibid.

(31) Shohaku Okumura, *Realizing Genjokoan*,120.

(32) Waddell and Abe, 35. See footnote 14 for the story about the name of Yakusan Igen (Yueh-shan).

(33) Nishijima and Cross, Book 1, 42.

(34) Ibid, Book 2, Komyo, 237-245.

(35) Waddell and Abe, 35.

(36) Nishijima and Cross. 43.

(37) Ibid., 43.

(38) Waddel and Abe, 36

(39) Ibid., 36.

(40) Nishijima and Cross, 44.

(41) Ibid.

(42) For further study on the law of cause and effect and Dogen, see Nishijima and Cross, *Master Dogen's Shobogenzo,* Book 4, Daishugyo, 43-53; Sanji-no-go, 115-125 and Shinjininga, 187-194. See also Steven Heine, *Did Dogen go to China? What He Wrote and When He Wrote it.* New York: Oxford University Press, 2006, 189-216, and Taigen Dan Leighton and Shohaku Okumura, *Dogen's Extensive Record, a Translation of the Eihei Koroku,* Boston: Wisdom Publications, 2004, Vol. 7. Dharma Hall Discourses 504, 508 and 510. p. 450, 452, 454-455.

(43) Nishijima and Cross, 44.

(44) Ibid.

(45) Ibid.

NOT DOING EVILS

Shoaku Makusa

Seisen Saunders

Dogen Zenji's teachings are a complex treasure to explore. Dogen is not writing about ideas and concepts. He is writing to free us from the prison we have built for ourselves out of our ideas and concepts. In his writings, he presents the experience of awakening. Therefore reading Dogen is a challenge. My suggestion is to read him like you would read poetry. Notice feelings and thoughts that arise, even though you may not be able to pinpoint how the reading provoked your response. Read Dogen as you would meditate. Be one with the writing and be aware of your feelings and insight. Then, gradually, you can find a thread to pull on and watch the living dharma unravel. In that spirit, I offer what comes up for me when studying Dogen's Shoaku Makusa. I make no claim that my view adequately reflects what he wished to convey.

I believe that Dogen gives us a treasure in this fascicle. That treasure is the practice of transforming evil into good (1).

Dean's Koan

During summer ango at Sweetwater Zen Center, a five-year-old child taught the assembly something he learned in kindergarten (2).

Friendship is wonderfully profound and infinitely subtle. There are "friendship moves" that deepen friendship. Friendship moves can be kind words, helping, sharing, etc. There are also "friendship blocks" such as saying mean things, hitting, and taking toys.

A friendship block can always be re-wound to unblock it. A person can point out that they gave out a block or received a block. In a re-wind, the people involved go back to the exact place where the block occurred. The person who blocked can say, "I'm sorry, I didn't really mean to do a friendship block. I meant to say 'what an interesting color choice' rather than 'you look funny.'"

The ango participants became aware of ways that we move towards friendship and how we block friendship. In examining how we block friendship, we were amazed at how often we do use unkind words and actions, and we noticed that we will change our behavior when it is pointed out. We decided that the first friendship block is an accident, the second block is on purpose, and the third block is a habit.

Dogen Zenji opens the fascicle "Not Doing Evils" with a poem from the ancient Buddhas.

Not doing evils,
devoutly practicing every good,
purifying one's own mind:
this is the teachings of all buddhas.

This poem is an expression of the threefold discipline (sangaku). The three parts of sangaku are precepts, meditation, and wisdom (3). The sangaku can be seen as a distillation of the eightfold path, which the Buddha taught as the way to end suffering. In this poem, not doing evils and doing good are about maintaining the precepts. Purifying one's mind is mental or samadhi cultivation and the teachings of all Buddhas is the cultivation of wisdom (4). Dogen tells us that this is the universal teaching of all Buddhas and we should all investigate it "with concentrated effort."

Dean's modern day koan also contains the points of the ancient poem. Friendship blocks are doing evils, friendship moves are practicing good, purifying one's mind is doing re-winds to realize friendship, and this wisdom is the teaching of all buddhas. It takes a seemingly impossible amount of mental discipline to catch friendship blocks and realize true friendship, just as the teachings of the ancient buddhas must be "investigated with concentrated effort."

The topic of evil is very relevant for our modern world. There are terrible wars raging around us. Many people, including veterans and the mentally ill, are without homes and living on the streets. Families are ripped apart by violence and hatred. We live in a world where over 100 million people live in extreme poverty and a child dies of starvation every five seconds (5). Our culture seems frantic to ignore the facts of the violence surrounding us. Most of us spend a lot of time blocking out reality with TV, smart phones, computers, drugs and alcohol.

Therefore, the question of evil is an extremely relevant question. How is it that we do not seem to get better? The war to end all wars continues to be the war we are in now. While sex and some kinds of love are banned, violence is the norm for our entertainment. We are shocked by nudity but love to watch violence. Perhaps, Dogen Zenji can help us understand evil and the way to end suffering. Since he lived during the violent Kamakura period in Japan, he was certainly acquainted with evil. It may be that one of the reasons Buddhism was established in Japan was due to unhappiness fueled by disunity and violence. So then, what is the salvation that Buddhism offers around "Don't do Evils"?

A list in Zen is not a hierarchal path. Therefore, these sangaku are not: first, don't do evil, then do good, then experience the oneness of all things, and then realize the wisdom of all buddhas. Instead every line of this poem is contained in every other. If you really see "Not doing Evils," you will realize what all buddhas realize. And, to whatever degree any part is cloudy, they are all cloudy.

In this ancient poem, the precepts are represented from two aspects: not doing evils and devoutly practicing every good. Nowadays, many Buddhists like to view the precepts from the positive aspect. For instance instead of practicing "don't lie" practice "telling the truth." Here Dogen looks at both aspects: the precepts from a proscriptive or what actions create suffering and from the prescriptive or as the medicine for salvation. When we practice the precepts, there are things to let go of ("don't do evils") and things to cultivate ("every good").

Many of us in the West were initially drawn to Zen when we heard of enlightenment. We felt stifled, stuck in a world of rules and shoulds, and embraced the teachings of non-duality. How liberating to see there is neither good nor evil and that everything as it is, is whole, perfect and complete. What a surprise it was, for me, the first time I witnessed people receiving the precepts. At the time, I was living in an "underground" community and one of the many ways we were disregarding the precepts was stealing food and things from local stores. Somehow, we justified that in a Robin Hood kind of way. When Maezumi Roshi asked those receiving precepts to promise "non-stealing", I was astonished. "You mean it's not ok to steal!"

Dogen Zenji says in this fascicle that in "learning of *anuttara samyak sambodhi* ... What one hears first is: 'Not doing evils.'" *Anuttara samyak sambodhi* is unexcelled perfect enlightenment. So Dogen is saying that the first step towards awakening to our true nature is through hearing the precepts. Moreover, he goes on to say "If one does not hear 'not doing evils,' one is not hearing the buddhas' true dharma but the talk of devils." Some may say that western Buddhism's early emphasis on oneness and disregard for the practice of "not doing evils" has created false views. I certainly recall that shocking moment ("you mean it's not ok to steal") as clear as a bell and clearly a changing point for me. I cannot remember when I first heard of the oneness of all things. Dogen says, "Know that hearing 'not doing evils' is hearing the buddhas' true dharma."

It is noteworthy that the ancients who wrote this poem did not start from samadhi or experience of emptiness (purifying one's own mind) but started with the precepts.

Dogen Zenji always emphasizes the "*Genjokoan*" or life koan. Our practice is our life and our life is our practice. In this fascicle he weaves together different aspects of practice (or life) to offer us a glimpse of true integration. His message is: don't be stuck anywhere! He does this from the standpoint of a number of Buddhist themes. Among those themes are: the three different aspects of precepts; the integration of relative and absolute; and how to see karma or cause and effect.

In the Zen tradition, we speak of precepts from three different perspectives. These are the literal or fundamental perspective, the relational perspective, and the one body perspective (6). Dogen moves freely among these aspects because in fact they are inseparable.

The literal aspect of following precepts is more like following rules. Just literally do what the precepts say. "Don't do evils" is simply don't do evils; "practice good" is simply practice good. From the literal standpoint, Dogen says, "In ...[the ancient poem] the term 'evils' refers to [what is called] morally evil among the categories of morally good, morally evil, and morally undefined. ... the term 'every good' refers to [what is called] morally good among the three categories of moral nature."

Dogen says: "The [meaning of the] phrase 'not doing evils' is not like what commoners first construe." Conventional wisdom tends to see morality from the literal standpoint. While easy to understand intellectually—just follow the rules—literally following the precepts is actually impossible to do. For example: I must kill (if only broccoli and nuts) to live. If I refuse to eat (to maintain the precept of non-killing), I am killing myself and disobeying the precepts. One of the reasons our life doesn't work is because we do not look deeply into the meaning of right action.

Dogen also talks about the relational aspects of "don't do evils" and "devoutly practicing every good." Evil and good are essentially relative, depending on place, time, and position. From the relational aspect, following precepts depends on circumstances. There are times when right action is stealing or lying. There are times when seemingly harsh words are actually loving words and

visa versa. From the relative view, there is no fixed evil
or good. By literally following the precepts, I may harm
others and therefore do evil.

> ...these three categories of moral nature encompass mani-
> fold varieties of dharmas. [The category of morally] evil
> encompasses: similarities and dissimilarities among evils
> of this world and evils of other worlds, similarities and
> dissimilarities among evils of former times and evils
> of latter times, as well as similarities and dissimilari-
> ties among evils of heavenly realms and evils of human
> realms. Even greater still is the divergence between the
> buddha path and the secular realm in terms of what is
> called evil, what is called good, and what is called mor-
> ally undefined.

In the same way, "devoutly practicing every good" is
relational.

> Because this is so, therefore, the good [performed by] some-
> one with the spiritual faculty for faith practice and the
> good [performed by] someone with the spiritual faculty for
> dharma practice will be vastly disparate even though the
> dharma is not different. It is just like how an auditor's ob-
> serving the moral precepts would correspond to a bodhisat-
> tva's violating the moral precepts.

How sad that, in our time, we are still fighting wars
over religious beliefs. It is so hard for us to see that the
heart of most faiths is love, even though the practices
are very different. From the relational standpoint
meditation, prayer, dance, or dialog are different
practices connecting to the same heart of our life. Our
lives are very different, and yet the basic fundamental
experience of life is the same.

This heart or sameness of our lives is the one body perspective of the precepts. Dogen says, "moral nature [of evils], however, is uncreated. The natures of morally good and morally undefined likewise are uncreated. They are untainted." The intrinsic nature of our life is no separation. From the one body perspective, there is no one to do harm and no one to harm. From this standpoint, we cannot break the precepts. Dogen says, "Good and evil are temporal, but time is neither good nor evil. Good and evil are dharmas, but dharma-ness is neither good nor evil. Sameness of dharmas is sameness of evil. Sameness of dharmas is sameness of good." Later he says. " Because the power of 'not doing' appears in full measure, evils themselves do not express evil, for evils lack fixed proportion."

It is very easy to be stuck in one of the aspects of the precepts. We become moral police judging the behavior of our self and others from the literal standpoint, we use the relative perspective to justify questionable behavior, and we fall into the complacency of being stuck in oneness. Dogen says, "to act on the assumption that 'if [evil already] is 'not doing,' then I can just do as I please' would be exactly as [mistaken as] walking north while expecting to arrive in Viet [i.e., in a southern region]." Dogen emphasizes the integration of all aspects of our life, so practicing precepts means integrating the three ways of looking at the precepts.

Throughout the fascicle, Dogen weaves the two aspects of realization, usually referred to as relative and absolute. The relative is all the differences that make up our life. The absolute is the oneness of all things. Dogen says that "not doing" is neither relative nor absolute since "not doing" is the non-dual.

It is not that evils do not exist, but that there is only "not doing." It is not that evils do exist, but that there is only "not doing." Evils are not emptiness; it is "not doing." Evils are not form; it is "not doing." Evils are not "not doing," for there is only "not doing." For example, spring pines are neither non-existent nor existent; they just are not done. Autumn chrysanthemums are neither existent nor are they non-existent; they just are not done. The buddhas are neither existent nor non-existent; they are "not doing." Pillars, lamps, candles, whisks, staffs, and so forth, are neither existent nor non-existent; they are "not doing." One's own self is neither existent nor non-existent; it is "not doing."

"Not doing" is practicing all aspects of our lives with no separation. Practice the three ways to look at precepts, the relative and absolute, form and emptiness, and good and evil as one. "Not doing" is not any of these and is all of these. This "not doing" is your true nature.

As we practice with our body and mind everything is called into practice. This is not a matter of rejecting body and mind, but practicing body and mind. We realize that this body is the body of all buddhas and ancestors, and as this body practices all Buddhas practice. We are holding our "four great elements and five heaps" (or five skandas) and releasing them at the same time. It all is the practice of "Not doing." Here nothing is defiled, nothing is evil, and nothing is obstructed. "Because the power of 'not doing' appears in full measure, evils themselves do not express evil, for evils lack fixed proportion. This is the truth of "one holding, one releasing": at that very moment one knows the truth that evil cannot transgress people and clarifies the truth that people cannot violate evil."

"In the practice of doing buddhas and ancestors, one's humanity is not violated, is not stolen, and is not lost. This being so, sloughing off finally comes." We do not reject our humanity, we do not reject our struggle with good and evil and in totally embracing it, it falls away. "One must practice through good and evil, causes and effects." This is the "one holding, one releasing" that he mentions.

In Dean's koan, the community realized that, becoming aware of friendship blocks, we can re-wind and cut them off. We also decided that the biggest problem with blocks is when they become a habit. We create patterns that keep us separate from each other because of our greed, anger and ignorance. Perhaps those patterns are what we mean by evil. Dr. Irvin Staub, defines evil as "intensely harmful actions ... and the persistence or repetition of such acts. A series of actions also can be evil when any one act causes limited harm, but with repetition, these cause great harm" (7).

One aspect of Zen practice is to see into and let go of our negative patterning. Dogen says, "There is no escape from regrets of having done what cannot be done. This too is [a result of] the power of concentrated effort on not doing." In practice, we see into the ways that we have stained that which cannot be stained. This is not to punish ourselves, but is the practice that unwinds our negative patterns. The Twelve-Step practice of making amends is an amazing way to practice "devoutly practicing." Doing the Steps, we see where we have harmed others and make amends for our actions. As Dean teaches, re-wind, go back to our error, make amends and move on. Acknowledging our patterns we can let them go.

Some practitioners believe that the way to true happiness or nirvana is to wipe out karma, or rise above karma. If I no longer have any mental or emotional patterns, then every moment is completely pure. This view sees escaping cause and effect as the way to end all evil. The famous koan, Hakujo's fox, looks at cause and effect in a different way. Hakujo says that the enlightened person does not fall into cause and effect and does not ignore cause and effect. Dogen says, "The original face of causes and effects is already clearly discerned: it is 'not doing,' it is uncreated, it is impermanent, it is not obscuring, it is not falling, it is sloughing off...Evils are not produced through casual conditions, for there is only 'not doing.' Evils are not extinguished through causal conditions, for there is only 'not doing.'"

In the same way, "Every good is neither produced through casual conditions nor destroyed through casual conditions... The causality of this good likewise is the fully apparent kôan of devoutly practicing. It is not a case of prior causes and subsequent results, but one of causes being fully perfected and results being fully perfected" (8).

Everything, including karma, is without separation. This does not mean that we can escape our humanness, our four elements and five skandas. It means that the nature of karma cannot be known, is without self. We must continuously practice seeing through our habits and releasing them (not falling into them).

Conventional wisdom views precepts as a straightforward description of cause and effect. If I do this, good things will happen to me. If I do that, bad things will happen. Dogen says, "Doing good is devoutly practicing, but it cannot be calculated. This devoutly practicing is living awakened vision, but it is not calculating. It does not fully appear for the purpose of calculating the dharma." He also says, "How pitiful are those people who merely know that evils are produced by causal conditions but who fail to see that those causal conditions in and of themselves are 'not doing.'" Often we may wonder, "Why did this terrible thing happen to me, I am a good person?" Or, we think, "Why am I so blessed when I have done harm to others in my life?" The fact is that we cannot calculate or understand karma. Dogen exhorts us to live in this moment. In this moment be "not doing," be no separation without hatred or clinging. "Devoutly practice" without calculation. He says, "Within the category of morally good there exists every good, but this does not mean that every good is fully apparent beforehand just waiting for a practitioner."

Dogen's view seems to be that, while we cannot ignore cause and effect we can see into the true nature of cause and effect, which is "not doing" or just this. Certainly practicing with our character defects, rewinding friendship blocks, and being aware of the consequences of our actions is practice. And, practice is realizing that the true nature of cause and effects is "not doing." What is this "not doing?" As long as we separate into subject and object (it is this or it is not that) we are doing evils. "Not doing evils" is letting go. Forget the self (as Dogen says in the Genjokoan) and just be.

Does this mean that we shouldn't act to stop evil? "Not doing" is not referring to passivity. We are not advised to become couch potatoes or hide in our rooms. Dogen says, "one holding, one releasing." "Not doing" refers to letting go of control. Release ideas, concepts and false self and just be. "Practicing every good" is holding on to what is good, without thought of where it came from or where it is going. Simply follow the good in every moment. This is right action. Just as, when we see a weed we pull it, when we see hungry people we feed them, when we see injustice we act. This holding and releasing is the opposite of passive. It means leading a vibrant, active life, letting go of false self and serving all beings. When we identify as anuttara samyak sambodhi or perfect enlightenment, then naturally we literally cannot harm others. Seeing myself as others and others as myself, there is no desire to harm. In the same way, we want to take care of others, as we want to take care of our self.

As I see it, Dogen is presenting "not doing" and "practicing every good" as transformational practices. There is a magical thing that happens when we practice "not doing evils." Once we hear this teaching as the true teaching of the Buddha, it begins to act on us.

> *Hearing it [not doing evils] like it is means [hearing it] as expressing words of unsurpassed bodhi. Because it is already bodhi talk, it talks bodhi. As unsurpassed bodhi's speaking turns into its hearing, one moves from the aspiration for "not doing evils" toward the practice of "not doing evils." As evils become something one is unable to do, the power of one's practice suddenly appears fully. This full appearance fully appears in measure as [vast as] all the earth, all the universe, all of time, and all dharmas.*

Simply by truly hearing "not doing evils" and practicing "not doing evils" an amazingly powerful transformation occurs. "At that very moment that very person, regardless of abiding in or traveling in places where evils are done or becoming involved in occasions for doing evils or becoming mixed up with friends who do evils, nonetheless will be unable to do evils."

In the same way once we begin practicing "devoutly practicing every good" a magical thing happens. Dogen says,

> *The myriad variety of good may be invisible, but they accumulate where one does good faster than a magnet attracts iron. Their power exceeds that of a vairambhaka tornado. All the karmic power generated [throughout] the great earth, the mountains, and the rivers in all the lands of the universe could not obstruct this accumulation of good.*

How wonderful and magical that when we practice "not doing" we become unable to do evils. And, how amazing that one good act creates endless good acts. It is like Indra's net, when we pick up one good all good comes with it.

"This kind of study is the kôan that has appeared fully and is the full appearance of the kôan." This is the "genjokoan" or life koan. Rather than escaping into some kind of pure samadhi removed from the world, this is the samadhi of oneness with our life, oneness with our karma. Totally practice not doing or just being here without anything extra and totally practice doing good or being one with my life.

> *...even though you do not obstruct [your own status as a] currently existing buddha and ancestor, you must carefully consider the truth of doing buddhas and doing ancestors throughout the twenty-four hour day as you walk, stand, sit, and sleep.*

This is our practice, rewinding, constantly examining our life. How to end evil is to be our lives. Completely be our "four elements and five heaps" or humanness. The fourth step (in the Twelve Steps) is "Made a searching and fearless moral inventory of ourselves." Fearlessly face our life including our character defaults and traumas. Courageously open up to ways we have been harmed and accept responsibility for the harm we have done. Not doing evils and practicing every good is like the serenity prayer.

> *God grant me the serenity*
> *to accept the things I cannot change;*
> *courage to change the things I can;*
> *and wisdom to know the difference.*

"Not doing" is acceptance, "practicing good" is changing and the wisdom is the "teaching of all Buddhas." Every moment has two aspects. We practice "not doing," accepting our life as it is. And, we take action towards good. We commit ourselves to the "path with heart" (9). Every moment we are recommitting and following the good. As we continue to commit to the "every good" path, all of our choices become "good" choices. We travel further away from "evils" and our life is content. More and more we are surrounded by good choices. Rather than living in right and wrong we see that there are several right answers to all occasions. Everywhere we look are good answers.

We are misunderstanding "not doing," if we think it only means totally accepting this moment as it is. Seeing our life from only this perspective is being stuck in the one body understanding of the precepts. Because Dogen embraces all aspects, following this practice on "not doing" and "practicing every good" means that we are able to see the intrinsic wholeness of our life and we are able to literally create a better life. Because our life just as it is is perfect, it is wonderful material to use to create the very best world possible.

Dogen only mentions zazen or Zen meditation once in this fascicle. "The occurrence of this full appearance is facilitated by completely seeing through 'not doing evils' and by eliminating them through sitting." He refers to "practice" throughout the fascicle. For Dogen the practice of zazen is the perfect manifestation of *anuttara samyak sambodhi*. I think, he assumes his readers are doing regular zazen practice. Obviously, mere intellectual understanding is not perfect enlightenment. However, in this fascicle, he is particularly emphasizing that the "not doing" that we experience in zazen should be being practiced every moment. Zazen is the very best way to realize "not doing evils" and "devoutly practicing every good" and that practice is in every aspect of our life.

Someone told me that Fr. Keating sees meditation as being "bathed in God's love." Keating says that we get the strength to explore our patterns created by our greed, anger, and ignorance from this love. Some of us may do zazen for years before we really begin to "study the self." This may be because our traumas are so large, and we have been afraid of them for so long, that it takes a long time incubating in "God's love" before we are ready to face them. Dogen sees zazen as the perfect manifestation of enlightenment and Keating sees it as "bathing in God's love." Either way, the practice of zazen gives us the courage to face our fears and do our searching moral inventory, which is "devoutly practicing."

In explaining "purifying one's own mind," Dogen sums up this fascicle to one paragraph. "Purifying one's own mind" is being here with no separation, and constantly practicing. We could look at these two aspects of every moment from the standpoint of the *Genjokoan*. "Not doing" is forgetting the self and "devoutly practicing" is studying the self.

> Purifying one's own mind" is not doing's "purifying," not doing's "one's," not doing's "own," and not doing's "mind." It is devoutly practicing's "mind," devoutly practicing's "own," devoutly practicing's "one's," and devoutly practicing's "purifying." Because of these reasons we say that "this is the teachings of all buddhas." ...Unless you study what all buddhas must be, you not only will be suffering for nothing but you will be a suffering human who is not even practicing the buddha path.

Dogen ends the fascicle with a koan:

Thereupon Juyi asked: "What is the Buddha dharma's great meaning?"
Daolin replied: "Not doing evils, devoutly practicing every good."
Juyi said: "If that is so, then even a three-year-old child could say so."
Daolin replied: "A three-year-old child maybe could say it, but even an elder in his eighties cannot practice it."
That being said, Juyi bowed and departed.

Intellectually anyone (even a three-year-old child) can understand "don't do evils" and "devoutly practicing every good." But, how many of us really practice it, practice our life as non-dual. How many of us have seen into the nature of all things, let go of ideas and concepts and devoutly practice being in the present every moment. Saying, "I am practicing non-duality," is not practicing it. How many of us can simply be in the world, naturally practicing "not doing" and "every good."

Dogen Zenji's words on this koan do not need any embellishment.

Juyi thought that Taolin was aware only of an existing mind's notion of saying that one must not act evil and that one must devoutly practice good. As for the buddha path's ancient, primeval "not doing evils, devoutly practicing every good"-this truth which transcends past and present-Juyi did not know it and did not hear it.
If you did not yet know the buddhas of the three periods, then how could you have known a three-year-old child?" "It is the utmost stupidity to think that a three-year-old child could not mention buddha dharma or that whatever a three-year-old child mentions must be easy. For this reason, to clarify birth, to clarify death, is the circumstances of the buddha family's single great affair.

The meaning of this saying is that there are words that can be spoken by a three-year-old child, and you must carefully investigate them. There are sayings that an elder in his eighties cannot practice, and you must concentrate your efforts on them. What a child can say is entirely entrusted to you. While this is so, it is not entirely entrusted to the child. What an elder cannot practice is entirely entrusted to you. While this is so, it is not entirely entrusted to the elder.

Many thanks to Dean, the five-year-old child, who gave us a modern koan which reflects the ancient wisdom. Realize true friendship, which is intimacy or non-separation. Practice "not doing" friendship blocks and purify your mind by rewinding and making amends when we do separate. "Devoutly practice good" by making friendship moves. This teaching from a child is the teaching of all the buddhas past, present and future.

Endnotes

(1) This chapter uses the text: *Treasury of the Eye of the True Dharma*, Book 31, Not Doing Evils (*Shoaku makusa*). Trans. William Bodiford, *The Soto Zen Text Project*, http://scbs.stanford.edu/sztp3/translations/shobogenzo/translations/shoaku_makusa/shoaku_makusa.translation.html.

(2) This teaching tool is described by Jennifer Kolari, *Connected Parenting*, www.ConnectedParenting.com.

(3) Prescriptive and Descriptive Approaches to the Threefold Discipline: A Response to Professor Ishigami by Carl Bielefeldt, Stanford University.

http://www.jsri.jp/English/BukkyoSymp/Papers/bielefeldt.html

(4) Private email from the translator William. Bodiford.

(5) The Statistics are from the Bread for the World website 3/10/2012. http://www.bread.org/hunger/global/

(6) Staub, E. The Roots Of Evil: The Origin Of Genocide And Other Group Violence. Cambridge: Cambridge University Press, 1992.

(7) Nakao, Egyoku. Zen Center of Los Angeles Jukai Book, Unpublished.

(8) This line is incorrect in the Bodiford translation. Bodiford sent this correction by private email.

(9) Castenada, Carlos. *The Teachings of Don Juan: a Yaqui Way of Knowledge*, Mass Market Paperback, 1976. Full quote: "Look at every path closely and deliberately, then ask ourselves this crucial question: Does this path have a heart? If it does, then the path is good. If it doesn't then it is of no use to us."

DOGEN'S SEVEN ARGUMENTS FOR EMPOWERING ZEN WOMEN

Raihaitokuzui

Grace Jill Schireson

Raihaitokuzui was written early in Dogen's teaching career (1240) (1) and represents the foundational teaching in Dogen's Zen that all beings, without exception, fully express Buddha nature. More specifically, in *Raihaitokuzui*, Dogen uses gender equality itself as an example of the complete expression of Buddhism in all beings. In 1240, Dogen was engaged in an attempt to build a community based on this very teaching. It was to be a community that not only taught equality, but also actually functioned based on respect for the equality of all beings, including women, as Buddhist teachers. Beginning with the Buddha himself, many great Buddhist teachers had to work around customs and laws of their times and cultures that placed women in the position of second class citizens (2). In this context, *Raihaitokuzui* was more than simply a statement of and about equality; Dogen wanted to go further to establish an actual community based on this teaching. Without enacting his understanding of equality in his community, full and true expression of the Buddha's teaching would be compromised.

Dogen's guidelines of equality for the Buddhist community directly opposed the established customs of his day. The guidelines he voiced and insisted on changed the lives of Buddhist nuns for more than 700 years and finally helped them to achieve equal status in the Soto Zen sect in 1989 (3). While Buddhist teaching and practice aimed to transcend gender discrimination, every practice place from the Buddha's time forward had followed local customs—usually misogynistic—that limited or forbade women from visiting sacred sites, leaving home, receiving the teachings or becoming independent teachers. In *Raihaitokuzui,* Dogen disputed such prejudices, superstitions, and prohibitions regarding women's ability to train and become full Dharma teachers, speaking not from a social justice perspective, but from the Buddhist perspective.

To fully appreciate the powerful and courageous nature of Dogen's teachings and the long-lasting effects of *Raihaitokuzui,* it is essential to understand how consistently women were excluded throughout Buddhism's history. While exceptional teachers bent rules to offer women training opportunities and full empowerment as teachers (4), few Buddhist leaders clearly branded these superstitions and discriminatory practices as contrary to the true spirit and intention of Buddhism. Perhaps the most remarkable point in *Raihaitokuzui* is its stress on the necessity of the actual rather than the conceptual inclusion of women as foundational to Buddha's vision of human actualization (5). Dogen took on the conventions of his time to establish a Buddhist teaching and community that could transcend the small-minded and prejudiced limitations of the day's Buddhist institutions, governments and local attitudes which even went so far as to deny women access to Buddhist sacred sites. In what follows, this commentary will focus on seven main points on which Dogen bases his argument for gender equality for teaching Zen.

The meaning of the title Raihaitokuzui

The translated title of Dogen's essay is *Attaining the Marrow, or Receiving the Marrow by Bowing* (6), a reference to a teaching from Zen's first Chinese ancestor Bodhidharma in which the marrow was considered the essence of Buddha's teaching (7). Focusing on these two actions – "receiving the marrow," and "bowing" – we can explore and understand Dogen's teaching about how to practice, with whom to practice, and what will inevitably result. To begin with, Dogen states that it does not matter whether a teacher is male or female. What's essential is that the teacher should be a person of "thusness." He quotes the Buddha on how to encounter such a teacher and not make personal judgments regarding the teacher's appearance, caste, or status. In describing this quality of a true teacher (marrow), Dogen implies that the teacher's realization is something palpable that the student must discern. This quality, this basis of the teacher's realization, is an expression of the essence or the marrow. Importantly, Dogen asserts that this quality is expressed equally and fully in both male and female teachers.

This first argument for fully recognizing women Zen teachers comes from Dogen's instructions on these essentials of practice; noting the palpable "thusness," a teacher embodies independent of status, gender or physical appearance. This first argument connects directly to Dogen's teaching "that all beings are Buddha nature." A conventional attitude that women are inferior beings interferes with seeing that all beings are Buddha nature, and limits the ability to recognize a woman teacher's authentic "thusness." In his second argument, for a practitioner to receive this "thusness" or "marrow," one must bow to the teacher's instructions. The ability to put a woman's instructions in command of a superior male position requires seeing past stereotypes, and must involve the active willingness of bowing. Dogen contends that finding a guiding teacher is the most difficult part of practice. It follows that excluding women from becoming one's teacher exacerbates this difficulty by narrowing one's options.

Regarding bowing, to receive the marrow one must cast aside judgments (of the teacher) and one's own importance. The entire transformation of ego and suffering is contingent on bowing to the teacher's instructions. In his second argument, Dogen explains that a student must perceive and accept that the Dharma has more weight than his/her own body, than his/her own life, or than any aspect of the teacher's appearance. In other words, as the student's ego arises in defense of him/herself from the teacher's Dharma instructions, the student must choose between his/her own (habitual or conditioned) way of doing things and the teacher's instructions that call for letting go, trust, and change. If the student cannot trust the teacher's teaching, "dharma is not transmitted to you, and you will not be able to attain the way" (8). Thus, this bowing to the teacher is an essential part of receiving the marrow. This bowing is not an outward form, but an inner willingness to trust the teacher's way and put aside one's own opinion. Here is the heart of Dogen's second argument in favor of men studying with female Zen teachers—a practice which contains additional challenges than studying with an easier-to-accept male teacher: To refuse to do so means one cannot put the needs of the dharma ahead of his/her own needs or negative cultural labels. According to Dogen, the inability to put aside one's own attitudes, and just bow to a teacher, makes attaining the way or realizing Zen wisdom impossible.

Dogen's examples of women teachers with male disciples

In the next section of *Raihaitokuzui,* Dogen recounts many historical examples of Buddhists who respected a teacher without regard to his/her/its appearance, tenure, status, profession, position or gender. Dogen narrows the field of these apparently discriminatory categories and devalued teachers down to just nuns and their accomplishments, and he points to the virtues of monks willing to receive teachings from these nuns. Because Dogen was fluent in Chinese and because he had studied in China, Dogen could draw on his experiences and his knowledge of Chinese historical *Chan* (Zen) literature for examples of female Zen masters and their exemplary male disciples. This was a particularly forceful argument in the newly forming Japanese Zen culture that looked to China for guidelines, admired Chinese culture, and believed in respecting and honoring Zen's Chinese ancestors.

In *Raihaitokuzui* Dogen cited two specific historical women Zen teachers, Moshan (ca. 800) and Miaoxin (ca. 880), both of whom had received their teaching empowerments from well recognized Chinese male teachers. He cited their teaching stories, which extolled their authentic "thusness," as expressed in their dharma words and actions. Herein we find Dogen's third argument in support of women teachers expressed (in the author's words): "Look, their teachings are indeed teachings of authentic Zen ancestors." Moreover, Dogen described and praised the men who recognized these women teachers and their consequent awakening upon receiving these women's teaching. Dogen found these monks' willingness to receive women teachers' "thusness" inspirational, and he confirmed the monks' awakening, under their women teachers' instructions, to be authentic.

Dogen praised these men as exemplars of the Buddha's teachings that denied the relevance of a teacher's status or caste. This is Dogen's fourth argument in favor of monks studying with women teachers. The monks he writes about were humble and sincere in following the Buddha way and they received realization in part *because* they were able to study with women. Dogen argued further that Japan's Chinese ancestors knew the true dharma and accepted and benefitted from women teachers, his fifth argument in favor of women Zen teachers was that this was the way of our ancestors. In his fifth argument, Dogen cites Sung dynasty practice as more developed and less hindered by cultural stereotypes. He encourages his readers to look to the Sung dynasty ancestors for inspiration and for instructions on how to practice more completely, particularly through recognizing women Zen masters as had been done in the past by Zen ancestors (9).

Buddhism versus Cultural Delusions

In the last section of *Raihaitokuzui*, Dogen put forth the most basic of Buddhist teachings to refute the exclusion of women as teachers, pointing out that we must not only put aside personal pride and prejudice, but also note the delusions of our own contemporary culture. Once again, Dogen expressed his teaching on the equality of awakening in basic Buddhist terms and in terms of how Buddhists should consider the common practices of their society in the light of Buddhist wisdom.

Dogen asked:

> *Why are men special? Emptiness is emptiness. Four great elements are four great elements. Five skandhas are five skandhas. Women are just like that. Both men and women attain the way. You should honor attainment of the way. Do not discriminate between men and women. This is the most wondrous principle of the Buddha way.* (10)

Dogen used the Buddha's teaching on no inherent self, or a self that is empty of permanent qualities, as an argument for equal rights for women long before the question ever arose in a political context. This was Dogen's sixth argument in favor of recognizing women Zen teachers. How much clearer could he be than "Emptiness is emptiness?" Making distinctions about women's nature or ability is not consistent with the teachings of the Buddha. He alludes to specific examples of monk's words or Buddhist texts that have been tainted with cultural stereotypes denying this basic truth—the self is inherently empty and refutes them for not being consistent with the Buddha way.

In *Raihaitokuzui's* seventh and final argument supporting recognition of women Zen masters, Dogen described how even Buddhist monks/sutras have been distorted, presumably by negative ethnic stereotypes about women from Hindu culture (11). First, Dogen referred to an Indian monk and the foolish beliefs of that era, going on to point out the Japanese exclusion of women from holy sites (in Japan, 1240) as a contemporary example of a similar cultural delusion that Zen practice should address.

> *There was a foolish monk who made the vow never to look at a woman, birth after birth, world after world. What was this vow based on—the worldly method, Buddha dharma, the outsider's method or the celestial demon's method?*
> *What is the fault of women? What is the virtue of men? There are unwholesome men and there are unwholesome women. Hoping to hear dharma and leave household does not depend on being female or male.*
> *If you vow for a long time not to look at women, do you leave out women when you vow to save numberless sentient beings? If you do so, you are not a bodhisattva. How can you call it the Buddha's compassion? This is merely nonsense spoken by a soaking-drunk shravaka.* (12)

Dogen labeled this ancient Buddhist monk and his vow to never look at a woman as drunken foolishness having nothing to do with the Buddha's compassion. Dogen was exposing this (and potentially similar passages) in Buddhist scriptures as cultural delusions outside the Buddha's way. For Dogen, such views of women as evil made no sense in the context of the Buddha's teaching. Dogen's comments on the practice of reviling woman as temptress pointed out that one cannot escape the "objects" that the mind reviles or fears. Such objects will always arise somewhere. Instead of banishing the objects that upset you, you must clarify your mind and not employ cultural prejudices as justifications for your aversion.

Dogen went on to point out comparably mistaken views in the Japanese Buddhist establishment of his own day, including the practice of barring women from the three holiest Buddhist sites in Japan —Mt Koya, Todaiji, and Mt Hiei.

> *There is one ridiculous custom in Japan. This is called a "secluded area" or a "Mahayana practice place," where women are not allowed to enter. This crooked custom has been going on for a long time, and people do not think about it.*
> *In the assembly of the Buddha since his lifetime, there are four types of disciples—monks, nuns, laywomen and laymen...Do not look for a secluded area that is purer than the Buddha assemblies that existed while the Buddha was alive.* (13)

This banning of women from Japan's sacred Buddhist sites was pervasive and continued for a long time (8th century to 1873 with the Meiji Reformation). The ban originated at temples that offered ceremonies to protect the state but spread far beyond to many other temples. It was based on a belief in purity and a fear of pollution (especially from menstrual blood). It was reinforced by older Buddhist views of Hindu origin about women's inferior nature (14). Given his views on the equality of Buddha nature, such Japanese superstitions about the dangers of women polluting Buddhist holy sites must have been particularly vexing to Dogen and his teaching goals. Dogen believed not only in teaching equality, but he wanted his (and other practice places) to function with equality for men and women. If women were forbidden to visit sacred Buddhist sites and temples, clearly, they could not receive the training they sought as Buddhist practitioners. The possibilities for women becoming fully trained and empowered Zen teachers were virtually impossible to achieve under the conditions of Dogen's day.

Perhaps it was the restrictions women faced and the widespread acceptance of these restrictions in the Buddhist institutions that inspired Dogen to write *Raihaitokuzui*. Even though his sermons didn't change the customs of his time, Dogen's words in support of women, based on the Buddha's timeless teaching, were used by Soto nuns in their twentieth century battle to win the inclusion and the equality that Dogen so passionately advocated in *Raihaitokuzui* in 1240. When Dogen put his sincere practice instruction into words, he had no idea of how they would affect women for centuries to come. He did not rely on philosophy or political views on governing to present his case for the empowerment of Zen women. His arguments for equality and inclusion, based on the Buddha's teaching and his own Zen realization, could not fail to ring true to the Soto Zen institution that had formed to honor Dogen's way.

We can now see the arc of Dogen's *Raihaitokuzui*, written when women were excluded from Buddhist practice places, forgotten for so many years, and rediscovered when it was time for women to take their places in the Soto Zen tradition he had created. May the importance of expressing our practice, in sermons, essays and deeds, continue to uplift all of us in the ten directions, throughout time.

Endnotes

(1) Levering, Miriam. "Dogen's *Raihaitokuzui* and the Fact of Women Teaching in Su'ng Dynasty China." *Journal of the International Association of Buddhist Studies* 21.1 (1998): 77-110.

(2) The Eight Special Rules were established around the time of the Buddha and placed the Buddhist nuns' order in a secondary position relative to the monks' order. The most senior nun was to be junior in status to the most junior monk. It is thought that the Eight Specials may have been necessary to satisfy opponents of women's full ordination in the Buddhist order. As a result of the Eight Specials, the nuns' order was seen as secondary and perhaps irrelevant and has struggled for recognition from then through today. Currently, the Buddhist Thai order today still opposes the full ordination of women based in part on the requirements established at the time of the Buddha.

(3) Arai, Paula K.R. *Women Living Zen*. NY: Oxford University Press, 1999. 73.

(4) Schireson, Grace Jill. *Zen Women: Beyond Tea Ladies, Iron Maidens, and Macho Masters*. Somerville, MA: Wisdom, 2009. In this text there are descriptions of many instances of male Zen teachers breaking the Eight Special Rules to teach and empower women disciples. These teachers include, but are not limited to: Bodhidharma, Joshu, Yuanwu, Dahui, Keizan, Hakuin, Man'gong, Yasutani, and Shibayama. All of these teachers made exceptional efforts to support women disciples, but Dogen's *Raihaitokuzui* is the only essay that presents the subject of gender discrimination as contrary to Buddhism itself.

(5) Levering's "Dogen's *Raihaitokuzui*" and Arai's *Women Living Zen* recount the inclusion of the nuns Ryonen (1231) and Egi (1234) in Dogen's early teaching efforts at Koshoji.

(6) Eihei Dogen. *Treasury of the True Dharma Eye, Zen Master Dogen's Shobo Genzo*. Ed. Trans. Kazuaki Tanahashi. Boston: Shambhala, 2010. 72-84.

(7) The title of this essay refers to the last interview Bodhidharma had with his four disciples wherein he described his disciples as having attained (in this order of depth) skin, flesh, bones, and marrow. Presumably, the marrow articulated by one of the disciples was the deepest expression of Bodhidharma's teaching. Therefore, marrow, represents the essence of Buddhadharma or the essence of Buddhist teaching.

(8) Tanahashi, 73.

(9) Levering explores the veracity of Dogen's claim about women teachers in her article Dogen's *Raihaitokuzui*. While there were recognized women Zen Masters, their situations were more exceptional rather than ordinary.

(10) Tanahashi, 77.

(11) At the time of the Buddha, Hindus believed that being born a woman was punishment for evil deeds in a previous lifetime. It was believed that women were evil temptresses and that they would need to be reborn as men to become capable of realization.

(12) Tanahashi, 80.

(13) Tanahashi, 82.

(14) See Groner, Paul. "Vicissitudes in the Ordination of Japanese Nuns." In: *Engendering Faith*. Ed. Barbara Ruch. Ann Arbor, MI: Univ of Michigan Press, 2002. 65-108.

ASTRIDE THE HIGHEST MOUNTAIN: DOGEN'S BEING/TIME, A PRACTITIONER'S GUIDE

Uji

Shinshu Roberts

Introduction

Uji, while often approached as a philosophical treatise of time's relationship to being, is a systematic exploration of time and being specifically intended to guide the practitioner toward realization. Dogen makes his intention clear when he states early in the text:

As evidence of their [hours in the day] coming and going is obvious, you do not come to doubt them. But even though you do not have doubts about them, that is not to say you know them. Since a sentient being's doubting of the many and various things unknown to him are naturally vague and indefinite, the course his doubtings take will probably not bring them to coincide with this present doubt. Nonetheless, the doubts themselves are, after all, none other than time. (1)

Dogen's point is that we don't look closely at the nature of being/time and if we do, we don't ask the right questions. If we did ask the right questions about being/time those questions would break open our understanding and lead to actualizing reality itself (2). We are so confused about how to approach the investigation of time in relationship to being, that we are groping in the dark. Our questions are the wrong questions and will ultimately not be productive. *Uji* is Dogen's attempt to lead us to productively and dynamically explore the true nature of reality through the lens of our being/time. He wants our doubt to become great doubt which in turn will lead us to great realization. Any other doubt is wasted effort.

Great doubt is a phrase in Zen Buddhism that describes a state of questioning which deepens our inquiry into the nature of reality. This inquiry will break open and free us from the ideas or unexamined ways that hinder us from fully engaging with our current situation. We drop all of our assumptions about what is happening. We finally see clearly without the filter of our preconceived ideas about what we would like to happen or what should happen. This freedom allows us to form new ways of thinking and being that connect us with all aspects of our existence. We take nothing for granted and respond fully and skillfully to life as it presents itself to us.

This essay is a discussion of the third of the six sections that make up Dogen's recipe for realization as presented in *Uji* (3). My intention is to help practitioners understand *Uji* not solely as an intellectual discourse on time, but as a practice guide whose purpose is to radically change our experience of *our* being/time as well as the being/time of *all* beings.

Practicing Being/Time: Am I a Buddha or a Monster?

In *Uji*, Dogen clarifies the practice of cultivating true understanding of time's relationship to being, which is *Uji* or time/being. Dogen wrote:

> ...*a person holds various views at the time he is unenlightened, and has yet to learn the Buddha's Dharma. Hearing the words "the time being," he thinks that at one time the old Buddha became a creature with three heads and eight arms, and that at another time he became a sixteen-foot Buddha. He imagines it as like crossing a river or a mountain; the river and mountain may still exist, but I have now left them behind, and at the present time I reside in a splendid vermillion palace. To him, the mountain or river and I are as distant from each other as heaven from earth.* (4)

In this passage, Dogen is writing about how we think about spiritual awakening as sequential time: that is, past, present and future presenting themselves in order. Hee-Jin Kim gives a very clear translation of the first line in *Flowers of Emptiness,* "Nevertheless an ordinary person untutored in the Buddha-dharma continues to have his/her own views of time" (5). In this case our 'own view' is

71

the common view that time and being are separate from each other. We think that time has some life outside of our experience of it and this is the time of past, present and future. Our tendency to experience time *only in this* way, is the problem. These 'own views' or limited views, are the views that we develop which hinder our clear understanding of the true nature of reality or being.

First we think that time is a continuous stream from past to future. Dualistically we think that our being is separate from the continuous stream of time. When we think this way, we tend to view our journey as beginning one place and time and ending at another place and time.

This way of thinking is the 'slightest discrepancy' that makes the Buddha Way "as distant as heaven from earth" (6). When we are slightly off in our understanding (for example we understand the words we hear but put them in the wrong context) then that 'slight discrepancy' will lead us off on a path that will not result in finding the truth of the situation. This results in the feeling that our activity and enlightenment are as 'distant as heaven from earth.' Yet heaven and earth are not separate and the way back is only a matter of hearing and understanding. It is all there in front of us (in and of us) all the time. Unfortunately, when we perceive our practice as off the mark, we think that we are a monster with three heads and eight arms, far away from the Buddha. Yet this is not so. Where is the 'Buddha' when we are in delusion? Where is the 'three headed creature' when we are 'a sixteen-foot Buddha'?

Dogen continues, "Hearing the words 'the time being,' he/she thinks that at one time the old Buddha became a demon and at another time he became a "sixteen-foot Buddha" (7). When we begin our studies we think, "Oh, I'm in delusion and I'm deluded about the nature of reality and if I do the right kind of training, I'm going to become a Buddha. Or at the very least be smarter than I was and have more wisdom than I had." When we are in delusion we think we are a demon and when we think we have attained some knowledge we are closer to being a buddha. This is the practice of the Buddha Way as a sequential passage from ignorance to realization. According to Dogen, this kind of thinking is a fallacy. In *Bussho*, Dogen explains:

> *If you wish to know the Buddha-nature, you must realize that it is nothing other than temporal conditions themselves. The utterance 'If the time arrives' means 'The time is already here, and there can be no room to doubt it.'* (8)

Here he clearly states that if we think our realization comes about solely due to a transition from ignorance to realization because of the passage of time training or practicing Buddhism, we are mistaken. Buddha-nature is time/being itself. Buddha-nature is not something that was once missing and now appears. It is always present. Buddha-nature is our essential nature and Buddha-nature is the essential nature of all beings. It is not separate from the time we experience right now. Our buddha-nature is another way of saying reality itself. Dogen expresses this when he states that Buddha-nature is 'nothing other than temporal conditions themselves." Buddha-nature/temporal conditions becomes *uji* or being/time.

The phrase Buddha-nature includes the particularity of one being (a person, animal or object) and all of Reality Itself. It is often used as a phrase pointing to the particular, since we usually attribute Buddha-nature to a person or thing. In actuality, reality is non-dual and in this case Buddha-nature refers to the interconnected, interpenetrating, cooperative and non-obstructed actualization of all being. Hence, Reality and Buddha-Nature are not two, they are descriptors of the same event. Time and being have the same relationship. Time is not separate from being. Being is not separate from time. Being is reality and time is reality.

Our realization and actualization of Time/Being, Reality or Buddha-Nature is enlightenment. This realization is embedded in this very moment. It is not potential. It is for this reason, Dogen emphasizes the simultaneity of practice and realization. Furthermore Dogen is very clear that we cannot actualize Buddha-nature without practice. In *Bussho* he writes, "A fundamental principle of the Buddha-nature is that it is not invested prior to attaining Buddhahood but incorporated upon attainment of Buddhahood. Buddha-nature and attainment of Buddhahood are always simultaneous" (9).

For this reason we must ask ourselves again, where is 'Buddha' when we think we are a 'three headed eight armed demon'? And where is the 'three headed monster' when we think we are a 'sixteen-foot Buddha'?

Time only expresses itself in the particularity of being, as emptiness only expresses itself through the particularity of form. This is why Dogen translates the characters for *Uji* as being/time (10). When we separate time from the specificity of a particular being, time becomes an abstraction. This abstraction makes us think of time as separate from ourselves. This is why we think of our practice as a means to get from here (delusion) to there (realization).

Dogen writes that we think our spiritual development is like crossing a river or a mountain: once we've gotten over the stream and climbed the mountain we will have arrived somewhere that no longer includes where we have been. This is a spiritual journey, right? We're crossing rivers, we're climbing mountains, we're doing all these kinds of activities that we imagine is the journey from our delusion to our realization, and Dogen says we then think, "But I have now left them behind." We make up our imaginary progress. We think in the past I was deluded and right now I'm somewhere along some imaginary continuum of practice leading to enlightenment. This erroneous continuum is based upon our initial understanding of the teachings.

For example your criteria might be that you can sit a seven day *sesshin*, or maybe you can sit zazen for 25 days straight. You think "I must be three-quarters of the way to enlightenment." Maybe you can dry towels with your body heat. You must be 90% along the way on the continuum. You have this idea about what the practice continuum is – so-called delusion to enlightenment – and where you are along that sequential line which delineates progress. Concurrent with this kind of thinking is the notion that once we are 'enlightened' we can't go back to delusion or that delusion is something in the distant past. Mistakes are behind us and perfection is in front of us.

When you view your practice in this way, you think, "Oh, well, I left behind all those mistakes because I'm here on my path to enlightenment. Dogen comments, "You imagine that you've left it behind and at the present time, you reside in the vermillion palace." The vermillion palace is the place of enlightenment. When you think that way, the mountain or the river is completely different from the place you are right now. Your struggles, the difficulties that you had, are something in the past and they're not currently in your present situation. This is Dogen's description of how we get caught in sequential/continuous time, especially when we think about the spiritual path. But do not only apply this teaching to spiritual practice, because clinging to this way of thinking is always a problem regardless of the situation.

Time is Multidimensional

> But the true state of things is not found in this one direction alone. At the time the mountain was being climbed and the river being crossed, I was there [in time]. The time has to be in me. Inasmuch as I am there, it cannot be that time passes by. (11)

The first line disabuses us of any ideas we might have that time is just about leaving the past, occupying the present and anticipating the future. Yet, he does not negate the reality of conventional time. There is no problem with using sequential time to get to work on time, plan a vacation, etc. The problem is when you develop preconceived ideas about what's happened in the past and what will happen in the future, in relation to your present moment.

In actuality when we are experiencing our present moment, we're experiencing our life, which includes "the time the mountain was being climbed and the river being crossed." We are simultaneously being all the individual times, all the individual being/times that we have experienced along the way. The elements of all the being/times make up each being/time and inform our experience. In other words, this moment *in* time holds all the other moments and times of your experience, including past, present and future.

This is true because each moment of our experience is part of a network of interconnected and interpenetrating being/times. Each moment also holds the past and future of this present moment. The future is not potential, it is really present now. This is not fate; it is the recognition that nothing can arise unless it is already present. You cannot make something from nothing.

Understanding our practice as *just this moment*, does not exempt us from the responsibilities of ethical behavior. Totally grounding oneself in time/being emphasizes our ethical responsibility because our moment to moment practice/realization is based in the fundamental truth of our interconnection with all being. If we think that we are enlightened once and never need to revisit delusion, then we are bound to become a wild fox. Living each moment totally includes all moments and all being. To think that it frees one from the snares of karmic and ethical repercussions is the response of the small mind and a complete misinterpretation of Dogen's teaching. In the mind of realization there cannot be a time when we do not include the whole of a situation and thus strive to respond with skillful means.

As egocentric humans we often forget that each moment of reality also includes the life of everything that is co-existent with our own experience. These co-existing beings are integral to our experience of reality, although we do not often recognize their function. Dogen writes in *Shobogenzo Zenki:*

> Life can be likened to a time when a person is sailing in a boat. On this boat, I am operating the sail, I have taken the rudder, I am pushing the pole; at the same time, the boat is carrying me, and there is no "I" beyond the boat. Through my sailing of the boat, this boat is being caused to be a boat—let us consider, and learn in practice, just this

moment of the present. At this very moment, there is noth-
ing other than the world of the boat: the sky, the water, the
shore have all become the moment of the boat, which is ut-
terly different from moments not on the boat. So life is what
I am making it, and I am what life is making me. While
I am sailing in the boat, my body and mind and circum-
stances and self are all essential parts of the boat; and the
whole earth and the whole of space are all essential parts of
the boat. What has been described like this is that life is the
self, and the self is life. (12)

In this example, Dogen is explaining that we are
making a boat a boat because we are defining the
boat's function – this object is functioning as a boat.
Yet, at the same time, this boat has its own being/
time which includes our presence and in this way the
boat is making us. Our presence is essential to this
moment, and this moment can be seen through the
experience of the boat or the rudder, the sail, the
sky, water or shore. From this perspective there is no
thing called boat or rudder or sky; these are labels we
give objects based upon our use or definition of that
object. In truth we are only part of the reality of the
boat. We are only part of the reality that we experience
from our own perspective. Simultaneously, all of reality
is experiencing this moment from its own perspective.
These various perspectives and interpretations do not
hinder the function of any one aspect.

For example, if you are attending a lecture, there is
the being/time of the chair you are sitting in. There
is the being/time of the podium. There is the being/
time of your shoes. There is a being/time of the other
audience members. So all of these elements — which
include the being/time of the bird we have just heard
outside – all of these being/times make up this moment.

And yet we are focused on a particular thing – our own experience. Perceptually, we're not able to hold all that is happening, yet it is happening, and it is making up the experience we are having, even though we are focused on only one aspect of the situation.

All of the particular dharma moments (moments of being/time) of each being/time is the accumulation of all of that is; all that you are. The whole of this universe makes up your complete life. As Dogen says, "I was there in time. The time has to be in me." In this way your life includes everything. As you expand this truth – this logic – you understand that our reality includes all time and all being, *at the same time* that we are experiencing a particular moment *in* time. It is a non-dual teaching about being/time which is quite simply the relationship that we have with all being. And we have this multi-faceted, multi-dimensional, interpenetrating interaction happening right now, at this moment. This continues in this moment and this moment and this moment and this moment. So that's what Dogen is saying. That's reality. That's the reality of our lives (13).

Furthermore, all the elements present in our being/time are helping us to *be* at this time. For instance, without the effort of the sun or plants or water we could not live. We could not sail a boat without the participation of the boat, the water, the oars, etc. All of these things we take for granted but they are the foundation of our activity (14).

Continuing with the paragraph from *Uji*, Dogen writes, "It cannot be that time passes away." Each present moment holds all being/time. Another expression used to talk about the present moment is the eternal now. As we actually ground ourselves in experience, our reality, this reality, this life, right at this moment, there is nothing else but this moment, and that is the eternal now. Each moment is this moment, eternally renewing itself as this moment. Eternal does not mean unchanging; it just means that it is eternally this impermanent moment, and this impermanent moment and this impermanent moment and this impermanent moment going on endlessly. In this way, we come to understand that time cannot pass away. It is the eternal presencing of our and all being/time. This eternal moment includes everything. Again it is not a moment that divorces us from interconnected causal relations, rather it is a moment that includes the totality of all existence and will be the genesis of our ethical enlightened response.

In the example given of climbing mountains and crossing rivers, each aspect of the journey is presented in each moment or step of that journey. The time of the mountain and the river are also part of the time of my being/time. Let's imagine you are actually walking through mountain ranges and rivers. The time of the mountains is your time. When you are there, that is your time. Just like the boat example from *Zenki;* you and the mountain are having a simultaneous experience of being/time which includes the being/time of each other, and simultaneously, the particular being/time of each individual expression of that moment. Our experience is not one-sided; it's just that as human beings, we tend to think about things exclusively from our perspective, not from the perspective of a mountain. In reality, we make up the mountain's being/time just as much as the mountain's being/time makes up our being/time.

Then you cross the river and when you're at the river, it also includes the time you climbed the mountain. The time of crossing the river includes the past of your experience of the mountain. If you assume that the time of climbing the mountain was past and crossing the river is the present, then you are leaving out the reality that climbing the mountain is still present in this moment. The moment of crossing the river includes the moment of climbing the mountain.

Everything is included. Each moment of our life includes the moment of all existence. This very moment of your life, includes the moment of the life of everyone else, for example somebody in Singapore. In this very moment right now, there is the experience that's happening in Singapore, or China or New York City that has some relationship to us even though we don't know what it is. This is the realization and enactment of the Bodhisattva vow to benefit all being.

At this point you might be thinking, "Oh, my gosh, my head hurts. How can I understand all of this?" Well, you don't have to understand all of this. We don't have to bring this forward into our mind all the time, but we do need to cultivate an awareness of true reality by recognizing our interconnection with all being. As we develop this kind of awareness of the spaciousness of the nature of reality – this inclusiveness of the nature of reality – then it allows us to include everything.

One reason we want to include this expanded view of time is to prevent us from concretizing the past. What is happening when we get neurotic about something? Something happens to us in the past. We hold on to it. At that point we have defined the experience we're having now based on something that happened in the past.

This is human nature. It's very difficult to avoid being caught by our interpretation of our past. If we can be in the present moment, and experience what is actually being presented to us in that moment without allowing that past, like a big wave, to wash over the present moment, then there's spaciousness in our response. Why? Because we are responding to what's actually happening. If we use the past as a tool to help us, then this is wholesome. But if we use past experiences to limit our response then this is a problem. Did you learn from a mistake in the past or did you learn to shy away from extending yourself? If you learned to avoid mistakes, then this is a problem because you are limiting your life. This is the nitty-gritty way this teaching works in our daily life.

Another way to understand the interconnected simultaneity of being/time is from an environmental point of view. What we do locally makes a difference globally. What's happening in China makes a difference to us in the United States. The amount that we drive cars or the amount that we misuse fossil fuels is going to or already has affected some other group of people or animals, the earth, and the environment.

These interconnected interpenetrating personal and global events are what we're being asked to be aware of. Once we become aware in this way, then the teaching starts to transform us. This understanding will strengthen and guide our aspiration to respond to each situation anew, with ethical and skillful responses. This is actualization of practice/realization. This is the mind of Buddha *just this moment.*

You can sit outside on a park bench and ask yourself, "What is the being/time of that person over there?" You don't know what it is. You don't know what they're thinking. But the willingness to be inclusive, the willingness to ask, "What is the being/time of a park bench? What is the being/time of that bird? What is the experience of this other entity that is in my being/time?" will expand your awareness of the inclusiveness of all of reality. Please allow yourself to contemplate and to include everything, instead of focusing on yourself, open up to the totality of life around you.

Every once in a while we go out into the woods and we take a big deep breath of air and hear the leaves in the trees, and we have this complete, holistic experience of being of this world. We say, "Oh, wow. I'm a human being in the world. I'm part of the universe." It's a great experience. But most of the time, we're saying to ourselves, "I've got to get somewhere. I've got to do this thing or that thing." Consequently, open inclusiveness gets lost in our life. Dogen's teaching is to stay grounded in the reality of our life just this moment. We need to wake up and cultivate this awareness. This awareness grounds us in the being/time of this moment.

When we can hold both the three headed, eight armed self centered me and still express the sixteen-foot Buddha of our true nature, when we can include the whole of the journey, then the vermilion palace is just this time/being of where we are right now. This *right now* includes everything and lacks nothing. This is the gateway to unobstructed practice.

Whose Time Is It Anyway?

As long as time is not a modality of going and coming, that time on the mountain is the immediate present – right now – of "the time being" (being/time). Yet as long as time takes upon itself a modality of going and coming, the being in me in the immediate now of the "time being" is being/time. So does not the time climbing the mountain or crossing the river swallow up the time of the splendid vermillion palace? Does not that time spit out this time? (15)

As long as we view time as more than sequential time our perception is filled with the now of our being/time. We don't view time as being past, present and future, and our minds reside in the present. This way of talking about time, as being completely present, is the being/time of non-duality. We drop the self and are thereby present without separation. We do have experiences like that.

For example, when you are so awestruck by the beauty of Yosemite National Park, you forget about yourself. You see this incredible vista and at that moment, you are completely one with everything in front of you, and you have dropped your "I." There's an awe of being completely present with all of presencing reality. That's the first sentence.

The next sentence "Yet as long as time takes upon itself a modality of going and coming, the *being* in me in the immediate *now* of the "time/ being" is being-time," describes time as both sequential and momentary. As time is 'marching on' in its sequential way, there is the subject "I am being" and the object of that being which is "the now." This experience is the experience of time being outside of ourselves, yet at the same time it is still the time of time/being or *right now*. No matter what we think is happening, reality itself (which always includes us) is happening, fully and unobstructed. We have the simultaneity of time taking upon itself going and coming (past, present, and future sequencing), and immediacy of our being/time.

Dogen cannot let us get caught in one side or the other. We are being asked to hold both views simultaneously. Both have their function and place. We cannot drop one view over the other, this is the middle way. If you deny that time has the element of past, present and future then you might think that you are free from the responsibilities of causal conditions. Yet, if you think that time is only past, present and future, you will be caught. You will be forever pulled around by your past experience/thoughts and future goals/ideas without grounding yourself in the present. So how does this work in practice?

Next he asks, "So does not the time of climbing the mountain or crossing the river swallow up the time of the splendid vermillion palace? Does not that time spit out this time?" Dogen's first point is when you're on a spiritual path or when you are experiencing your daily life, it is in each step that you have realization. In this way, each step swallows up the vermillion palace; it swallows up the goal. Our experience is the experience of this moment, not the experience of some future event. This is immediate time 'swallowing up' the goal, in this case, the goal of enlightenment.

Upon arriving at this goal – the vermillion palace, the end spits out every step that you've taken to arrive at this place. The 'end' includes and is the result of each individual step. Often we think when we have reached some place we have designated as a goal, we are no longer the person we were before attaining the goal. But this current person still includes the past person. Simultaneously, this 'spitting out' is happening in each moment, because actually there isn't any place to arrive and there isn't any place to have been. The place we're arriving is a point in time we designate as 'arrival.' How can we say what arrival is except through our own (or someone else's) determination of 'arrival'?

How can we say where the beginning is unless we say it's the beginning? Is birth the beginning of our life? Is death the end of our life? Let's say death is the end of consciousness, certainly as we know it, but our bodies continue. Our atoms and molecules continue: there is some continuum, there's something that's ongoing. Life's transformation doesn't just stop. So this birth, this event designated as birth and this event we call death are only points along a life continuum. Dogen is saying that in each moment we are on this journey of our life, or in this particular example, this spiritual moment, in each moment that moment swallows up the designated goal, the thing that we've called enlightenment.

Let's say your idea of enlightenment is that you're going to be perfect. You're never going to make any mistakes. That's often our idea of enlightenment, which is a very interesting idea because it basically means we think life will be a lot easier for us. That's what we really want. It's not that we want to be perfect, actually; it's that we just don't want to struggle anymore, so we think somehow that is what enlightenment means. But if we pay a lot of attention to each moment of our life, then that idea gets lost. The moment swallows that up, because what we're paying attention to is what's happening right now in our life. We forget about this thing called perfection and we just live our life with the tools that we have in that moment of living our life. This is a key teaching in Dogen's understanding of actualizing realization.

There is no Vermillion Palace. Shunryu Suzuki Roshi supposedly said about enlightenment, "Be careful what you wish for because you may not like what you get. You may not get what you think you're going to get"(16). Of course you couldn't possibly get what you think you're going to get. We couldn't possibly, because no matter what your idea is, it's just an idea. Reality, as each moment happens, swallows up the vermillion palace. By the time we get to the moment we thought was going to be the moment of arrival, it's just another moment. It's just another step. That step spits out every step that's happened before it. That arrival spits out or includes everything that preceded it.

To swallow something has two connotations. To swallow means to make something disappear. In this way the goal disappears in the time of now. Swallowing also leads to digestion. When you digest something, you chew it up, you swallow it and when you spit it out, you regurgitate it.

Regurgitating something means it has already been mixed up. There is a sense of incorporation, if you will. It is no longer recognizable as what it was. There is this constant reciprocity going on, things are happening simultaneously; the swallowing, the chewing, and the spitting up is all happening simultaneously in each moment. Dogen is admonishing us to stay focused on what's in front of us and not get caught up in some idea about the future. That's our mandate as practitioners, as people. So please leave your delusion behind and let go of your preconceived ideas about what enlightenment is going to look like or what your life is going to look like.

We can also get caught when we say something is right and wrong. This is just another kind of sequential thinking that leaves no room for multi-dimensionality. Your ideas are being expressed as this or that. Things are right; things are wrong. It behooves us to think about this teaching in ways that are flexible, more generalized. We want to say to ourselves, "How does thinking about things in a sequential way block me from truly being present with what's actually happening?" For example in a difficult situation, you can explore your experience of suffering by wondering what is blocking you from having a mind of ease. You might say, "Hmm, how is this? Am I caught in some kind of thinking that's very sequential and narrow? Is there some way that I can think about this that's really more inclusive, that's more of a round shape rather than a straight line?" That's a way to work with the teachings of being/time.

What is Today's Time?

The creature with three heads and eight arms is yesterday's time. The sixteen-foot Buddha is today's time. Nonetheless, the nature of the truth of this yesterday and today lies in the time when you go directly into the mountains and look at the myriad peaks around you – hence there is no passing away. So even that three-headed, eight-armed creature makes a passage as my being/time. Although it might seem as if it were somewhere else far away, it is the time right now. The sixteen-foot Buddha-body also makes a passage as my being/time. Although it might seem as if it were somewhere else over there, it is the time right now. (17)

Dogen continues to talk about the spiritual path (which is also our daily life). Yesterday's time, the three heads and eight arms, is delusion. The sixteen-foot Buddha, or realization, is today's time. When we think about having attained some wisdom, we think delusion is yesterday's time and our current wisdom is today's time. Nevertheless, Dogen writes, "The nature of the truth of this yesterday and today lies in the time when you go directly into the mountains." Going directly into the mountains is a way of talking about true realization.

Going directly into the mountains is being present for your life just as it is. When you go directly into the mountains, and "... you look at the myriad peaks around you..." your view is 360 degrees. This 360 degree view is a view that includes the sixteen-foot Buddha and the three headed eight armed demon. You understand that each moment contains both delusion and realization.

"Hence," Dogen says, "there is no passing away." In this moment of being present for what's actually happening (going directly into the mountains), this inclusive present includes everything that came before and everything that is happening now. All these different activities are happening simultaneously, interpenetrating; in this moment. There isn't any passing away; this is the eternal now, this eternal presencing of all of reality.

Dogen continues, "So even that three-headed, eight-armed creature makes a passage as my being/time." He's saying this is part of your being/time: delusion is included. It's all right here, right now in this moment, and it's not a problem. Even though it seems like realization is over there—on some idea we have of the path, we realize it's right now in the midst of our confusion. When we can include everything and just be this moment, then we are fully engaged and free.

Imagine a circle is the present moment. This present- moment- circle has everything that has happened within it, all of your experiences. How will you leave the circle of the present moment? Imagine that in this present- moment- circle, you could have 360 choices of how you will exit that moment. You have a myriad of action choices that might best suit the experience at hand. But you are caught on a particular preconceived idea from the past, like "I am bad, I always do this thing in this moment." Or, "This is the right way to do this!" Or "This person I'm talking to is always such a problem."

For example, you're having a difficult interaction with somebody, with whom you have had unpleasant experiences and you don't like them. These concretized past moments really narrow down the scope of how you're going to respond to that person. If you could be present with that person, you might notice that they were frightened, or that they seemed like they were in pain in some way. Suddenly you feel compassion for them rather than aversion.

You may notice something about them that might also be true about you. You might notice that actually there are some similarities between you and them and then the situation is more open and your response more spacious. The moment this happens you have utilized all 360 degrees of the present moment. In that moment you're giving yourself the tools and the responses to be able to exit that moment any number of ways. When we respond to the moment that is actually happening – not our idea of the moment – then we are completely expressing this moment.

Standing on the mountain of the present moment is actually being able to see what is happening, and is realizing that this inclusive now is your being/time, too. You realize that being/time includes everything in that moment. It includes peace and war; it includes calmness in the midst of chaos. It includes realization in delusion. It includes your compassion in the midst of your anger; all of those things are there. This is realization. This is simultaneously swallowing and spitting out of reality.

Hearing the Truth of Time

> *Hence, pine trees are time. So are bamboos. You should not come to understand that time is only flying past. You should not only learn that flying past is the virtue inherent in time. If time were to give itself to merely flying past, it would have to leave gaps. You fail to experience the passage of being/time and hear the utterance of its truth, because you learn only that time is something that goes past.* (18)

"Hence, pine trees are time. So are bamboos." All of existence is included in each being/time, not just our particular perception of self/other. Time and being exist together – in the particularity of life. Pine trees, bamboo, rivers and mountains are all existence being/time.

Nothing is left out. Everything is participating in making our reality as we are making their reality. It is each entity that makes up the totality of our world. There is no such thing called time outside of the particularity of the being/time of each person or thing.

"You should not come to understand that time is only flying past. You should not only learn that flying past is the virtue inherent in time." To understand that time has another aspect other than flying past, is to say that time is connected to being. We may think time is outside of ourselves flying by like a bird, but this is an illusion. Time resides within each being and is experienced by each being. At the same time there is the impermanent nature of our experience of time/being.

How do we actually perceive time? If you take away a clock, if you take away the mechanical devices that we use for measuring time—how do you know what time is? How do you experience time? You experience time through impermanence. You experience time through change. It is the cyclical changes of the sun making its cycle through the sky, the moon moving through the sky, the stars; that's the basis of what we call sequential time or conventional time. Clock time is based upon one aspect of sun/moon time.

But we also experience impermanence in our body. We look in the mirror and we understand about the passage of time. Often in Zen we are admonished to pay attention to the fleeting nature of our existence. This line acknowledges this aspect of practice, but teaches it is not enough.

Time is flying past, yet everything has its own being/time. Time cannot exist outside the realm of being. We are time. We are impermanence. If you see time as outside of yourself, if you don't understand time as being something that's an integral part of your essential being, yet also inclusive of all being/time, then there's going to be a gap.

What is the gap? The gap is the missing present which unifies this fleeting time passing. Often when we focus on what is next or what has happened we do not inhabit this presencing moment. This moment is the glue of our practice/realization.

From a personal point of view, the gap is that you're not present. The gap is, for example—and we've all experienced this gap—you're driving your car along a familiar route and you're thinking about something at work and you have no memory of how you got from point A to point B. You don't have any conscious memory of driving that stretch of the road. Of course if something out of the ordinary happened, you'd wake up and pay attention to the road, but there will be a gap.

There are actually gaps in our life. When we are not present for our life, there are gaps. Dogen is reminding us if you just live in sequential/continuous time, if you're just always thinking about the past and planning the future you let those thoughts define your present and then there are gaps. Consequently you will be living your life in that gap. You are not experiencing the actuality of your being/time. This actualizing moment is the glue of being/time. For this reason Dogen writes, "You fail to experience the passage of being/time and hear the utterance of its truth because you only learn that time is something that goes past."

Realizing and examining this habitual way of thinking is a primary way to wake up to our life. "You fail to experience the passage of being/time and hear the utterance of its truth." Time/being, as it is expressed in this moment, in this body, is speaking to us right now and time/being is everything. Time/being is the particularity of each thing, which in turn makes up the totality of time/being. It makes up the universe, and the universe in each thing is saying, "Hello, hello, hello. This is reality. This is true. Be with me, please. Live this life with me. Live your life. Wake up." This is a wide open gate to realization that Dogen is trying to get us to investigate.

The Essential Point

The essential point is: every entire being in the entire world is each time an independent time, even while it makes a continuous series. Inasmuch as they are being/time, they are my being/time. (19)

We are citizens of the being/time of all being/time, and the being/time of all being/time is citizens of us. I use the word 'citizen' because it denotes the shared activity and responsibility we share with all beings for this world. In *Shobogenzo-Gyoji* (Continuous Practice), Dogen writes:

Because of this continuous practice, there are sun, moon and stars. Because of this continuous practice, there are earth, sky, and heart within and body without.... Conditional arising is continuous practice....The time when continuous practice is manifested is what we call 'now.'" (20)

This is another aspect of the 'essential point' of being/time. When my being/time is the shared being/time of all being, we enter the territory of shared reality and responsibility. My continuous practice and the continuous practice of all beings are not different, just as my being/time and the being/time of all being are not different. In *Gyoji, Bussho* and *Uji* (among other fascicles) Dogen unites realized activity and being/time as one unit of actualization. We and all beings make the world. "We set the self out in array and make that the whole world" (21).

We cannot escape the interpenetrating effects of our activity which resides in the 'now' of our being/time. Realizing this interlocking and interconnected simultaneity of activity, responsibility and being within the context of the present moment is the essential point. "One must learn in practice that unless it is one's self exerting itself right now, not a single dharma or thing can either immediately manifest itself or make a passage" (22). This is a theme that Dogen returns to over and over again.

We are not separate from this simultaneity of arising being/times. To see the world only from the side of your needs and desires is delusional. But when we can allow everything to come forward in the moment and present itself to us, and to actually see it, standing on the mountaintop, having a view, that is realization.

Yet, we cannot get trapped in trying to manipulate and force this actualization. We don't always know what is happening. Again, quoting from *Gygoji,* "When the continuous practice which manifests itself is truly continuous practice, you may be unaware of what circumstances are behind it..." (23). We can only present our understanding as it arises within the context of our present circumstances. How we respond is often spontaneous. Our practice is to focus on the immediate awareness of our life. In this way, we can truly look at our circumstances and the circumstances of others.

In concrete terms waking up to this moment, which includes the other, means that we are willing to drop our own agenda. If we are having a difficult conversation, we clearly look at the other person and respond to their suffering. Dogen's teachings must be taken out of a rarified context and applied to the 'real world.' Dogen's intention was to write about reality in such a way that we are forced to deeply penetrate the truth of this moment. Yet, that can only be manifest in our daily lives. This means "Inasmuch as they are being/time, they are my being/time...." refers not to some abstract idealization of practice, but to the difficulties we have with our neighbors or co-workers. This too is the essential point.

We enact this teaching by realizing our shared continuous practice with others and our skillful response is not hindered by problems. We can only do this practice within the present moment. We use the past as a source of learning, not as a way to reify our position. We use the future as a finger pointing at the moon, not as a fixed notion of success or failure. Each moment is a fresh moment that we can enact to the best of our ability. Each moment is another birth of continuous practice. This is our being/time. This is the shared being/time between us and all beings. Again, this is not abstract. It must be enacted while we wait in line at the supermarket or drive to work. We do not need extraordinary circumstances to actualize our realization – right now. We cannot waste a moment.

Endnotes

(1) Eihei Dogen. "Uji," *The Heart of Dogen 's Shobogenzo.* Trans. Norman Waddell and Masao Abe. Albany: State University of New York Press, 2002. 48-49.

(2) Joan Stambaugh briefly addresses this question of correctly doubting in *Impermanence Is Buddha-nature: Dogen's Understanding of Temporality.* Honolulu: University of Hawaii Press, 1990. 27.

(3) The six sections of *Uji Shobogenzo* are: 1. Introducing a definition of being/time, 2. How to approach our understanding of being/time, 3. The relationship of sequential time and present moment, 4. How being/time is totally expressed, 5. The continuous practice of being/time and 6. Realization and being/time.

(4) Waddell and Abe, 50.

(5) Kim, Hee-Jin. *Flowers of Emptiness: Selections from Dogen's Shobogenzo.* (Studies in Asian Thought and Religion v. 2): Lewiston/Queenston: Edwin Mellen Press, 1985. 225.

(6) Waddell and Abe, "Fukanzazengi," 3.

(7) This is a reference to the opening verse of the fascicle: "For the time being, I'm three heads and eight arms" (For the time being, I am in delusion) followed by "For the time being, I'm eight feet or sixteen feet." (For the time being, I am realized.) This is the simultaneity of being realized and deluded at the same time. No being/time obstructs the being/time of our myriad experiences. Waddell and Abe, 48.

(8) Waddell and Abe, "Bussho," 66.

(9) Ibid., 73.

(10) Waddell and Abe: (page 48, footnote 1) The two Chinese characters *u-ji* used in the opening verse of the fascicle mean "for the time being" or something is happening "at a certain time" or "sometimes." Dogen changes this meaning to being/time by reading each character separately. *U* is read as being and *ji* is read as time, instead of the combined and more common meaning of "at a certain time."

(11) Waddell and Abe, 50.

(12) Eihei Dogen. "Zenki," *Master Dogen's Shobogenzo*, book 2. Trans. Gudo Nishijima and Chodo Cross. London: Windbell Publications, 1996. 286.

(13) This interpenetrating, multidimensional, constantly changing, non-obstructive dynamic view of reality is China's contribution to the Buddhist doctrine of non-duality. From the Hua-yen and T'ien T'ai schools, Chan Buddhism and consequently Japanese Buddhism inherited and developed this expanded view of reality.

(14) Hee-Jin Kim writes about this dynamic while discussing the fascicle *Shobogenzo Gyoji*. "The total exertion, as the ascetic dimension of a single dharma, is expounded as the act of absolutely and thoroughly enacting the entire world with the entire world: the self-exertion of the entire world in and through itself. For this reason, the total exertion comprises not only mere human efforts on the part of an individual, psychological, intellectual, moral or otherwise, but more importantly, the totality of self/world and Buddha-nature. In this respect total exertion is that stereological act in which a single dharma is chosen and enacted not dualistically but non-dualistically. In other words by virtue of its total exertion, a single dharma is no longer one among all dharmas, but the total dharma that is all there is in the universe." Kim, Hee-Jin. "Existence/Time as the Way of Ascesis: An Analysis of the Basic Structure of Dogen's Thought." *The Eastern Buddhist*, 10/1978:57.

(15) Waddell and Abe, 50.

(16) This is often quoted at San Francisco Zen Center. I do not have a source for the quote.

(17) Waddell and Abe, 51.

(18) Ibid.

(19) Ibid.

(20) Cook, Francis. *How To Raise an Ox*. Los Angeles, CA: Center Publications, 1978. 176.

(21) Waddell and Abe, 49.

(22) Ibid., 54.

(23) Cook, 176.

GREAT REALIZATION

Daigo

Byakuren Judith Ragir

There is a great question: "What is awakening? What is enlightenment?" What is this experience we seek, as silver-tongued great master Joshu says, "like Buddha-seeking fools"? There has been great controversy over this question and how to manifest realization for a couple thousand years between different schools of Buddhism. Many chapters of Dogen's *Shobogenzo* attest to the importance of this question in Dogen Zenji's teaching and in his subtle exposition of *practice-enlightenment,* and none more dearly than in the fascicle *Daigo* (Great Realization).

Practice-enlightenment or *practice-realization* is a phrase that is imminent in Dogen's writing. He is particularly adamant that we see all things from a non-dualistic perspective, which is the underlying principle of Zen. But often our supposedly non-dualistic point of view is still sticking to one side like glue! We contemplate over and over "Not one, not two." It is a paradox. From Dogen's point of view, we can't understand enlightenment as a "thing" or an "event in time" that opposes or erases the ordinary perspective of life. Hee-jin Kim expresses this paradox as a "foci" (1). "Foci" is used instead of the words: antitheses, polarity or opposites. It is the dynamic interplay between the two poles of daily life and enlightenment or the absolute and the relative. They are interdependent and have no independent self-nature. They are intertwined and dynamic, swirling around the foci of the present moment. Kim writes,

> *The ultimate paradox of Zen liberation is said to lie in the fact that one attains enlightenment only in and through delusion itself, never apart from it. Strange as this may sound, enlightenment has no exit from delusion any more than delusion has an exit from enlightenment. The two notions need, are bound by, and interact with one another.* (2)

1.

Often the first paragraph of a fascicle is the summary of the whole fascicle. Here is the first paragraph of *Daigo* using Okumura Roshi's unpublished translation:

> *The great Way of the buddhas has been transmitted intimately without interruption; the diligent activities of the ancestors have been manifested extensively in ordinary lives. Therefore the great realization is manifested; the Way is reached through no-realization; reflecting realization and freely utilizing the realization, losing realization and letting the practice go. This is the day-to-day activities in the household of the Buddha-ancestors. The very moment of great realization is now!* (3)

The Merging with the great functioning of the moment is the great reality and our enlightenment. It is constantly transmitted in each moment of time and form in our daily life. It is none other than our daily life: *grasses, walls, tiles and pebbles.* The illumination of daily life is revealed when we no longer grab onto the illusion of a centralized self: a *me or mine.* Without a *me or mine,* (which is a realization unto itself; the digestion of no-centralized-self), the Way is reached through *no-realization* or no seeking of a future-Buddha but the wholehearted expression of the present moment. Katagiri Roshi, my root teacher, taught that the merging of subject and object, i.e. the relinquishing of the "me-subject" into the total working of this very moment, is enlightenment.

Some other translations illuminate this paragraph with certain phrases that I find helpful.

- Nishijima and Cross translate, *"transmitted intimately without interruption"* as *"a continuous line of immediacy"* (4).
- Nishijima and Cross translate, *"freely utilize"* as *"to play with realization."*
- Kazuaki Tanahashi uses the phrase, *"enlightenment disappears in the practice of letting go."* For the line: *"and letting the practice go"* (5).

The translation *"intimately without interruption"* comes from two characters put together. One means cotton ball, that which cannot easily be pulled apart. And the other is the character for "sacred" or "intimate" (6). Cotton is an example of intimacy and because it can't be pulled apart, it is like practice/realization or delusion/enlightenment.

Okumura Roshi said that the line, *"The Way is reached through no realization"* is the main point (7). This is an example of reversing what the Heart Sutra calls upside-down thinking or inverted views. This "no" is not negative. This "no" is a pointer at that which is not bound by time and space and pervades the whole universe. This "no" is allowing non-substantiality and impermanence to reflect (like the moon in a dewdrop) in every moment and every object. This "no," in and of itself, decomposes so-called *"enlightenment."*

2.

Going on to the next lines of the text:

> *This is the day-to-day activities in the household of the Buddha-ancestors. There are twelve hours that (Buddha-ancestors) hold up and utilize, and there are twelve hours that (Buddha-ancestors) let go and are utilized. Furthermore, there is playing with mud-balls and playing with spirit that jumps over this pivotal point.* (8)

Where is the household of the Buddha-ancestors? It can be none other than right here and now, manifested through our *practice/realization,* through the complete connection to this moment. The Buddha-ancestor's household is our house and our actions. It is the living vitality of these chairs, sofa, table, books in this very library I see in this moment. The 12 hours are the ancient Asian clocks equivalent to our 24 hours. Enlightenment is expressed through and only through the day-to-day activities of our life. How could it be otherwise? Where else could it be expressed? Could this, as some people misconstrue, only be expressed in zazen in a formal situation in the zendo?

The dharma wheel turns through this dynamic of inter-being: doing and receiving, holding on and letting go, or holding up and utilizing. We are utilized by the "Whole Works" (*Zenki,* another fascicle in the *Shobogenzo*) in both are taking up and doing, and we are utilized by the "Whole Works," in our letting go and non-doing or our receiving. So we can push the dharma wheel by our conscious activity and we receive back the response from the universe by the wheel moving us. This is playing with form and emptiness. This is playing with doing and non-doing. This is the pivotal point or as Kim calls it, the "foci," which is the swirling interplay of the opposites.

One of Zen's traditional images is the Bodhisattva covered in mud. Because an enlightened person has to and does live in the world of form and samsara, we cannot help but be covered by mud. From a non-dualistic point of view, mud and cleanliness (purity) interact and are different sides of the moment. A misunderstanding of Zen practice is to aspire to live in the pristine, transcendent world of enlightenment that is separate from delusion. The teaching of *Daigo* is the counterpoint to that misunderstanding. In Zen reality, we wade into the swampland and we are unafraid of the entangled briars of life. We are able to do this playfully because at each moment we open up and see the moment as an expression of universal play *without moving a speck of dust or destroying a single form* (9). This means that the form world remains complete, "as it is," even though our perception of it has been transformed. Through this process of pivotal awareness, we are able to be clear. We can serve others with a clarity and understanding of life that can actually help. We are not holding on to the three poisons that grow out of the idea of a separate self. We are light-hearted, supported by boundless openness, while we play in the mud of samsara.

Let us investigate now the common notion of realization as an "event" that occurs in space and time usually in a formal Zen setting. We often say that this is a *kensho* or an insight into the truth that happens in a moment. Zen students often spend their time obsessively looking for this experience and missing this actual moment of "total dynamic working" (another translation of *Zenki*) as it is, which is the present moment. This is why Dogen coined the term *practice/realization* as a remedy for searching. We can settle into the "self" in this very moment. With *practice/realization*, each moment, however we evaluate it, good or bad, right or wrong, *kensho* or delusion, is the form of that moment's realization. Seeing our life in this way, we begin to stop seeking for somewhere else and make peace with what is occurring right now and open up to the moment as "just this." *Like a fish swimming in water, like a bird flying in the sky* (10), we humans are always in the field of realization. It is our home.

3.

Oddly enough, there is a story of Dogen's 'moment' of enlightenment even though he has written extensively against seeing realization as a singular event in time. The story of his enlightenment is now controversial amongst Zen scholars. Even though we have this legendary enlightenment story, Dogen's subtle expression of the teaching, his exposition of *practice/enlightenment*, seems to be much more extensive and many faceted than a moment in time. He exposes how we experience a realization, how we use this realization, and how we forget this realization.

This story was taken from the biography of Dogen written by Keizan Jokin Zenji in the *Denkoroku, Transmission of Light*. The story is:

> *A monk fell asleep in the meditation hall. Tendo Nyojo (Rujing) shouted at the sleeping monk: "True zazen is the dropping off of body and mind, why do you sleep?"*
> *These were turning words for Dogen.*
> *When he was greatly awakened, He went to the abbot's room and bowed with incense.*
> *The abbot Nyojo: "Why do you offer incense?"*
> *Dogen: "Body and mind have dropped off."*
> *The Abbot changed the order of the words and verified Dogen's enlightenment: "Dropped off body and mind."*
> *Dogen: "Don't approve me lightly, this is just a temporal ability."*
> *Abbot: I am not approving you without reason.*
> *Dogen: Why then?*
> *Abbot: You dropped off body and mind.*
> *Dogen bows.*
> *Abbot: You have dropped off dropping off.* (11)

Today some Dogen scholars, such as Sugio Genyu of Yamaguchi University and Ishii Shudo of Komazawa University, think Keizan put together this story arbitrarily, using certain aspects of the oral story of Dogen. Otherwise Dogen's criticism of practice aimed at attaining *kensho* only becomes a contradiction to his own teaching (12).

Professor Ishii has said that the fictitious story of Dogen's enlightenment experience has caused more misunderstanding of Dogen's teaching than any other fabricated portion of Dogen's biography (13).

It seems more accurate to trust the description that Dogen himself wrote in *Hokyoki, Record of the Pao-ch'ing*

Era. "Dropping off body and mind" is the teaching Dogen received from his teacher Tiantong Rujing (Jap: Tendo Nyojo) and is at the heart of his own teaching. According to the *Hokyoki*, he had several dialogues with Rujing about this phrase over a period of time. It seems that these dialogues with Rujing elucidate more what Rujing meant by "dropping off body and mind" than the legendary story of a momentary event of insight.

In one of these teaching encounters, Rujing said, "Sanzen is dropping off body and mind" and "dropping off body and mind is zazen." Katagiri Roshi translated Sanzen as "practice" elucidating the phrase *practice-realization*. Katagiri writes:

> *Sanzen is zazen. Usually sanzen is translated as practice. But in English, practice doesn't hit the mark of what sanzen is. Literally, sanzen means to surrender ourselves to tranquility or simplicity in life. Simplicity is manifested only when our life, our circumstances, are very clear. ......Living in the complicated world, how can we manifest or understand simplicity? This is a difficult matter for us, but we have to do it because it is our original nature. So everyday we try to practice. In order to submit to tranquility or simplicity in life, we do zazen. Simplicity is zazen. Zen Buddhism sees or hears or understands the world and human life as action that is constantly going on. Dogen Zenji particularly mentions that, under all circumstances, we should understand the human world in terms of the flow process and not in terms of concepts.* (14)

This "simplicity" of Katagiri Roshi might be what is left after dropping off body and mind. It is the simplicity of the world "just as it is" with the dynamism of the absolute and relative intertwined in "this very moment."

In his lecture on *Bendowa*, The Wholehearted Practice of the Way, published in Eihei-ji's magazine *Sansho* in July 1999, Suzuki Kakuzen Roshi wrote:

> *In the case of Dogen Zenji, his religious experience is not attaining some sudden and special psychological satori experience. Dogen never talked about such an experience in Shobogenzo. In his teachings, realization is a deep awareness of the fact that the existence of the self is not a personal possession of the self.* (15)

Enlightenment is not something "a person" possesses or achieves. In truth, the pivotal point is that enlightenment happens when the world no longer revolves around the false sense of a permanent self. Our minds are quiet. The interdependence of the physical body is seen. The existence of a solidified independent unit of the body unravels. We join in with the universal functioning of the moment and lose the "I." This happens in zazen and it can also happen in a more active version in our daily life.

In daily life, our surrender to the moment and its corresponding single-minded activity break open our "stories" or the "worlds" we conceive. We begin to understand that any moment's activity is inherently enlightened. The idea that our form of life is "bad" or to be "transcended" or that it is "just a delusion" drops away. The form that appears in this moment is life itself. Our mental fantasies about the moment can be dropped, but even our mental fantasies are not outside of the mystery. They are the mystery of our brain's excretions and of being a human. These ancestors pointed out that each moment, event, person or thing IS the eternal source. How could it be otherwise? There is no mystery outside of this one moment's manifestation. It is verified in humans by doing this one moment's activity, dropping off body and mind with no *me or mine*, and becoming one with our activity. Going back to the first paragraph: Daily life *reflects realization*, we are able to *freely utilize the realization*, and *realization disappears through the act of letting go.*

What is it exactly that we drop off to achieve what Katagiri Roshi called simplicity or things just as they are? Rujing told Dogen in one of these dialogues that dropping off is being freed from the five desires and six coverings (16). The five desires are the grabbing on that comes through the five senses (seeing, hearing, smelling, tasting, touching). The six coverings are similar to the hindrances: greed, anger or hatred, sleepiness or dullness, distraction, doubt, with the addition of ignorance. With all our coverings dropped off, our naked being, interpenetrated with universal energy, is what is left in simplicity and in activity.

Last, here is an excerpt from the third conversation recorded between Dogen and Rujing in the *Hokyoki*:

> *Rujing: Buddhas and ancestors practice many virtues, generation after generation, and allow their mind to be flexible.*
> *Dogen made a prostration and then asked, "What does 'allowing the mind to be flexible' mean?"*
> *Rujing said, "Affirming the dropping off of body and mind of the buddhas and ancestors is the flexible mind. This is called the mind-seal of the buddhas and ancestors."*
> *Dogen made six prostrations.* (17)

I am more and more intrigued with what a "flexible mind" means and its relationship to enlightenment.

Dan Brown, a contemporary Tibetan teacher, calls it "a serviceable mind" (18). This mind is non-distractible and clear. It does not grab on or reject. It meets. It meets each and everything as Buddha. It takes care of each and everything as Buddha because it sees the truth of the mystery of life in each phenomena arising. The ancestors call this flexible mind like a pearl in a bowl, freely able to move in an unending flow in any direction with no obstacles.

To summarize Dogen's encounters with Rujing as written in the *Hokyoki*:

1. Practice (sanzen) is dropping off body and mind. Dropping off body and mind is zazen.
2. Dropping off is being freed from the five desires and six coverings.
3. Buddhas and Ancestors do not forget or abandon living beings in their zazen; they offer a heart of compassion to all.
4. Affirming the dropping off body and mind of the buddhas and ancestors is the flexible mind.

4.

The next section of Daigo is an acknowledgement of the variety of practitioners that exist and that human capacity is greatly varied. But he admonishes us: *Among these types of people, don't regard one as sharp and another as dull. Various types of people, as they are, actualize various types of accomplishments* (19). Dogen doesn't espouse the stepladder or developmental approach to realization. Nor does he want us to evaluate and discriminate one kind of practitioner as better than another kind of practitioner. *All these different types of practitioners must bring forth great realization and thereby realizing afresh the state of great realization. The time which is just the moment of this (realization) is now* (20).

In the text he acknowledges four types of knowing:

1. Innate knowing – born with the ability to penetrate life, knowing through understanding and seeing life.
2. Learned knowing – gotten through study and practice. "Study the self."
3. Buddha's knowing – neither innate nor learned, going beyond time and space. Touching the network of all beings. "Forget the self."
4. Knowing without a teacher –Dogen's use of this phrase is that the teacher and student have become one and therefore the student no longer relies on the teacher (21).

We do not practice to attain enlightenment but we practice within enlightenment. We manifest great realization through our activities, our doing and non-doing, moment by moment. With 100% mind and body together, focusing on what we are doing, forgetting the self, we carry out great realization. We do this again and again in the current moment.

5.

The great master Rinzai said: "In this great country of Tang (China), if we look for even one single person who is without realization, it is difficult to find one."

This section continues to break apart the idea that there is a "person." What is the meaning of *"even one single person?"* Dogen unravels the concept that personhood is a "thing." It brings forth the Buddhist main teaching of no-centralized self. *Who* realizes or does not realize enlightenment? The question is not so much "realization" but the investigation at the core of realization, which is the "who." Dogen is questioning here, what is realization with no fixed identity, and how does that express itself in our moment-to-moment life of phenomenon arising?

Dogen can be relied upon to try and trick our brain through his semantics and the changing of syntax. He could be called a twentieth century cubist. He tries in one paragraph to present and unbind all the different angles or views of an object. None of these different views are "right." It is like Nagarajuna's quadralemma. It is not this and not that. It is not both or not neither. Where then do we reside? Beyond thinking and language. In showing all the angles and contradicting all the opposites, he dismantles our notions of solidity, independent identity and linear time. He encourages us to open our minds beyond our concepts and fixed views, and experience just this moment as it is realized.

Here again in this koan, there is a play on words in the meaning of "no realization" or "without realization." *"If we look for even one single person who is without realization, it is difficult to find one."* Is Rinzai or Dogen talking about the impossibility of finding a "single person" because there is no independent personhood? A single person cannot be found at all! Or are they saying all people, whether they have insight or not, have inherent realization, and therefore it's difficult to find a person who is "without realization." Or are they talking about a Buddha/person who has entered into the realm of "letting go of their realization and leaving no trace?" These people are, indeed, very difficult to find.

Dogen continues: *This statement by Rinzai is the skin, flesh, bones and marrow of the authentic stream, which is not mistaken (22).*

Dogen brings forth his view that enlightenment doesn't have levels or a step-ladder-approach-to-realization by bringing up the metaphor used in Bodhidharma's transmission. If we believe that there is a realization that will take place in the future, we end up constantly leaning into the future and believing that a future moment will be "better" than this moment. This leaning into the future is actually absurd, if we understand the teaching that Katagiri Roshi expounded in his phrase "Each moment is the Universe" (23). Leaning forward, we actually miss realization itself.

Dogen uses the story of Bodhidharma to illustrate this point. Bodhidharma had four students and with each one he said, "You have understood my skin, you have understood my flesh, you have understood my bones and finally, you have understood my marrow." He did actually transmit to the student, Hui-k'o, who had understood his marrow. But in a non-dualistic teaching, what is the meaning of surface and deep, skin or marrow?

I have always enjoyed the pointing out of Master Joshu in this koan:

> *The master Joshu instructed the assembly saying: "Kashyapa transmitted it to Ananda. Tell me, whom did Bodhidharma transmit it to?"*
> *A monk asked: "Supposing that the Second Ancestor 'got the marrow', what about it?"*
> *Joshu said: "Don't slander the Second Ancestor."*
> *And then Joshu added: "Bodhidharma had a saying, 'Someone who is outside attains the skin; someone who is*

inside attains the bone.' Tell me, what has the one who is inside attained?"

The monk asked: "What is the truth of 'attaining the marrow'?"

Joshu said: "Simply be aware of the skin, where I am, the marrow is not established."

The monk asked, "What is the marrow?"

Joshu said: "In that case, the skin too is sought and not found." (24)

This koan takes apart the metaphor of skin, flesh, bones and marrow. It disassembles this imagery because in the deepest truth (the marrow), there is no substantiality and that "no solid thing" crosses all the boundaries in all four levels. In the marrow's view, there is no skin and there are no layers. Each layer is the expression of the mystery itself. Each moment is complete. The surface of ordinary life is still the full expression of inter-being and the absolute. But if you understand the marrow, you will look for the skin and not find it. Of course, in the discriminating form world, we still have all four layers of the body undisturbed by oneness, as any surgeon will testify. Respecting the world of this and that, undisturbed by oneness, Bodhidharma did not transmit to all four students; he still, only transmitted to the person who had the marrow. Illustrating again "Not one, not two." But even though the skin and the marrow are different in our differentiated world, there is actually no real "value" difference in terms of essence.

Using this collapsed metaphor helps us break down all the 'stages' we experience in various understandings. The different facets of enlightenment are seen from a cubist view as different angles of the same thing and expressed by Dogen thus:

1. The Great realization is manifested (*kensho*).
2. The way is reached through no-realization—emptiness—(beyond conceptualization and disappearing in the practice of leaving no trace).
3. Reflecting realization and freely utilizing realization (returning to delusion or utilizing realization in form).
4. Losing realization and letting the practice go (Being fresh in each moment and then the next, being fresh in the flow of time).

Deep and shallow, realization and delusion, are bound to each other and pivot around each other dynamically. We cannot separate one from the other. We cannot "realize" through our discursive thinking, which always discriminates into categories and then compares. This is why we practice letting "thinking" go through concentration. *How do we think of not thinking? – Non-thinking* (25). We "realize" through letting go of our discriminations and preferences. We see interdependence as a non-verbal knowing.

In this same section Dogen writes: *"In the great country Tang" means "within the eyeball of the self"* (26). The country of Tang – China – is a vast geography. In the ancient time, it was the entire world. The entire world is reflected in the eyeball of one single person. The eyeball of the self is the gate of inside and outside. Each single person is part of the entire network of interdependent co-origination. Each eye, person, knot, or jewel is at the intersection where the ropes of Indra's Net meet. If you pick up one knot, the whole network responds and moves. So, is there even one single person who doesn't move with the whole of Indra's Net? The separation of I and other is dropped off. The single eye has become the whole universe. The eye can become really large

- two or three great countries of Tang. We simply live in the movement of the whole Net. The whole universe or the dusty realms of samsara do not limit us.

Dogen has such a wonderful way of encouraging people. He knows how difficult practice is and how much human beings compare and discriminate. He uses the metaphor of a half a person in a number of fascicles. This phrase, a half a person, is a very compassionate way to deal with and acknowledge the difficulties and inconsistencies of our practice.

Dogen writes:

Even if it is difficult to find a single person without realization, there is half a person who is without realization and that person's face is gentle and peaceful, imposing and dignified; have you seen such a person? ..... We should try to find two or three great countries of Tang within one person or half a person. Is it difficult or not? When we have such an eye of insight, it is possible to say that we have been filled with the dharma of buddhas and ancestors. (27)

I have two ideas on what a half person might mean. First, it is all of us humble practitioners who do not hit the mark 100% of the time: half on, half off. Second, is the middle way. It is the person who is able to integrate the relative and absolute. We are both, our human selves with all our foibles AND our absolute selves which sees the boundless. Katagiri Roshi called this our "total personality." This half person or perhaps this single person is the practitioner who has brought together the boundless and the particular. That person will have a face that is gentle and peaceful, imposing and dignified. This is the manifestation of the mysterious workings of a spiritual life. An "I" does not control it. Realization has disappeared and the person has disappeared and just activity is left.

6.

Great Master Baozhi (Hochi) of Huayan (Kegon) temple in Jingzhao (Keicho) (Dharma Heir of Dongshan, his personal name was Xiujing), was once asked by a monk: "How is it when a person of great realization returns to delusion?" The master said: "A broken mirror never reflects things again. Fallen flowers never go up the tree." (28)

How is it when a person of great realization returns to delusion? Here is another way that Dogen is trying to break apart our notion that realization and delusion are dual. Is there a separate place other than our here and now that houses great realization? *Is there?* With this question, we seek to penetrate how delusion and enlightenment are one. Synonymously, we could also investigate form and emptiness as one. Dogen is repeatedly pointing us to the truth that the moment of phenomena arising and the boundless universal energy function together. The great realization is seeing that oneness without ignoring their twoness.

Our usual commonplace notion is that the development of enlightenment has a starting point, a process, and a result. In our ordinary minds, we see enlightenment as the result and zazen as the means or cause. Dogen encourages us to see cause and effect as one, and to see form and emptiness as one. He also encourages the opposite. Dogen will counter and break up this traditional instruction, by also saying: *form is form and emptiness is emptiness.* We honor oneness and we honor differentiation. They come together in the form of gassho, the left hand meeting the right. They are one whole and yet different. Like a leaf falling from a tree, first you see the front of the leaf, and then the back of the leaf, but still, it is one whole leaf that falls to the ground.

"*How is it when the person of great enlightenment returns to delusion?*" It is like the 10th Ox-Herding Picture, "Returning to the marketplace." The world is born anew and we enter the dust and briars of the thicket of samsara. Delusion becomes the field for our enlightened expression. Manifested reality is the practice place of enlightenment. Dogen writes, *As there is a person of great realization, there are buddhas of great realization; there are earth, water, fire, wind, emptiness of great realization; there are exposed pillars and lanterns of great realization* (29). The elements, the trees, grasses, and pebbles, the concrete objects of life, are all, also, Buddha beings.

The line that most informs this intertwining of form and emptiness is: *We should know that there is great realization that makes 'returning to delusion' into the most intimate partner* (30). Delusion and great realization are intimate partners! They need each other and they are actually inseparable.

"Returning to delusion" is "identity-action" written about in Dogen's fascicle, *Bodaisatta Shishobo*, The Bodhisattva's Four Methods of Guidance. Identity-action means to lose our personal identity by merging with the activity of the moment. We have to become the object and the object becomes us. In that intimacy, we know true interdependence. All the objects in the form world can begin to teach us about themselves. We can truly listen to the mystery of the world. We have a continuous sense of awe in this mystery. This is how an enlightened person re-enters the world of delusion, discrimination and separation.

Katagiri Roshi writes:

We have to see everything in equality but that doesn't mean there is no difference. We have to see equality, but not in the realm of equality; we have to see equality in the realm of differentiation. Differentiation must be formed not in differentiation, but in equality. Then, differentiation and equality are working in identity action. Identity action does not function in a small area called ego, but in the vastness of existence.

When we clean a room, we just clean the room. The room is not something different from us. We are the room, the room is us. Then we and the room communicate with each other in the rhythm of identity-action. We have to take the best care of the room we can, because the room is not a material being apart from us. The room is a great being called Buddha-dharma. Buddha-dharma means the unity of Buddha and us, Buddha and the room. " (31)

With this as our understanding, we become very flexible and fluid. When oneness arises, we are completely absorbed in non-differentiated oneness. When a form arises, we become 100% the functioning of that form or that moment. It is not 50% and 50% (32). In that sense, it is not the middle way between delusion and enlightenment. The middle way is actually 100% either this or that. But in the background, we know that they mysteriously influence each other, moment after moment.

Each moment/form/event is an arising from the whole network of karmic conditions rather than an "I" making a "thing" happen. Because this dynamic functioning cannot be stopped, cannot be identified by a certain "name" or "sign," it goes beyond the notion of a "moment" or a "thing"; it is the eternal source itself.

This koan's question, *"How is it when a person of great realization returns to delusion?"*

The koan's reply, *"A broken mirror never reflects things again. Fallen flowers never go up the tree."*

Our human stories are always broken and we are often shattered. As humans, we are and always will be covered in mud. This is the deeply unsettled human predicament. There is an inherent human tragedy and that is our death and all the losses along the way. We attach to our children and then we have to let them go. We attach to our life and our accomplishments and then illness comes and we have to let them go and die to our world. The small deaths we experience every day are broken mirrors and fallen flowers. They are the expression of the pivoting of life and death. Impermanence and insubstantiality is totally obvious in the world of delusion. *Nothing is hidden* (from *Tenzo Kyokun*, in *Eiheigen Zenji Shingi*). In delusion, noticing this insubstantiality is enlightenment.

We become aware of the true nature of reality. *Great realization of this present moment is neither the self of one's own nor the self of others; it does not come from somewhere else, there it fills in ditches and also fills up in valleys* (33). This realization fills the smallest ditch and the largest valley with boundlessness. *Because the broken mirror is truly nothing other than a broken mirror* meaning that life and death, appearing and disappearing, are always present and totally spinning around each other. *No matter how many concrete activities are actualized, all of them are equally the reflection of never-again-reflecting* (34) which points to emptiness or no-realization never-again-reflecting. This is the equality of oneness. Different than the traditional "mirror wisdom," this is the *no-realization* that doesn't reflect anything at all.

To return to delusion is to forget unity and realization and see the uniqueness of each phenomenon. *Losing realization, and letting the practice go.* Or, *Enlightenment disappears in the practice of letting go.* We need to be free from realization. Being free from freedom (35), we can come back to the world of discrimination and live in the world of discrimination without any clinging. We experience our stories freed from the charge of our desire system that centers on me and mine. The "I" is filled with "other" but the forms of the world appear the same.

As we return to the world of delusion, we cannot ignore the laws of the form world. We cannot reverse time, even though, strictly speaking, there is no time. There is no before and no after. Each object or event has its own dharma position. Fallen leaves do not go back on the tree, nor does ash turn back into firewood. A seed of a rosebush does not produce a magnolia tree. The karmic functioning of the form world is exactly as it is. The differentiated world cannot be ignored or obliterated, but must be vividly experienced and understood for what it is. Returning to delusion is practicing forever (36). Bringing the hand of emptiness and the hand of form together in a bow.

7.

The last koan in this fascicle is:

> *Master Mihu (Beiko) of Jinzhao (Keicho) let a monk ask Yangshan (Gyosan), "Do people of nowadays still need realization or not?"*
> *Yangshan said, "It is not that there is no realization, but what should we do about falling into the second head?"*
> *The monk returned to Mihu and reported (Yangshan's answer). Mihu deeply appreciated it. (37)*

In finishing the fascicle, we come back to Dogen's original question when he first went to China. If everything is Buddha or imbued with realization, why practice? Or why try this hard to realize the truth? Or, in other words: *Do people today still need realization or not?* Can we use the whole treatise on "delusion and enlightenment are one" to support a side that says we don't need to realize the dharmakaya? *Yangshan said, "It is not that there is no realization, but what should we do about falling into the second head?"*

In this imagery, the first head is the head of realization, which is completely quiet, still and beyond discrimination. We could say, the second head is the head of discursive thinking and duality. The second head has two heads. One is the "monkey mind" which is filled with our fantasies and our desire system and its preferences. The mind of the "I." Another second head is the mind that approaches the form world, sourcing itself from the organizing principles of no-centralized self and interdependent co-origination. This second head sourced from the first head begins to express enlightenment with whatever arises, black or white. In that case, the second head is also *satori.* With this understanding, we begin to make true contact with life. The first head and the second head dance with each other intimately.

Dogen writes:

> *It means that the second head is satori. To mention 'the second head' is like saying 'Do we become satori?' 'Do we attain satori?' It means that saying either 'to become' or 'it is coming' is satori. Therefore, although it seems that Yangshan regrets falling into the second head, he says that there is no second head (that is separate from the first head.) The second head made out of satori is, simultaneously the true second head. Therefore, even though it is the second head, or even the hundredth or thousandth head, it is nothing other than satori."* (38)

Dogen doesn't suffer from the fear of falling into the second head. He includes the second head in enlightenment. He brings all of who we are: the present, the past, and the future selves together; he brings our darkness and our light together, into the essence of any given moment.

Dogen admonishes us to contemplate: *Do we rely upon realization or not? We must investigate these words quietly; we should replace our heart with them and replace our brain with them* (39). Do we source our life from realization or not?

8.

If we listen to Dogen's teaching, we do not become "Buddha-seeking fools." He implores us not to *vainly wait for realization to come.* He encourages us in this very moment to express *practice/realization* as the means and the end. The two notions of delusion and enlightenment, *need, are bound by and interact with one another.* They have no beginning, middle or end. They have no separate place. *The day-to-day activities in the household of the Buddha-ancestors,* is our house, our life and our activity. This doing and non-doing, is imbued thoroughly with the total dynamic functioning of moment-to-moment reality. Nothing is left out, and there can be great peace and ease in this understanding. Even though realization is the experience of great, whole oneness, Dogen ends this fascicle by saying, *The head of great realization is black; the head of great realization is white* (40).

This article is inspired by the lectures of Shohaku Okumura Roshi and supplemented by the years of listening to Dainin Katagiri Roshi talk about Dogen Zenji. To these wonderful teachers, I am greatly indebted. All misunderstandings are my own.

Endnotes

(1) Kim, Hee-Jin. *Dogen on Meditation and Thinking: A Reflection on His View of Zen.* Albany, NY: State University of New York Press, 2007. 4.

(2) Ibid., 1.

(3) Okumura, Shohaku. *10th Chapter of Shobogenzo: Daigo (Great Realization).* Unpublished translation draft used at the November 2008 Genzo-e.

(4) Eihei Dogen. *Master Dogen's Shobogenzo, Book 2.* Trans. Gudo Nishijima and Chodo Cross. London: Windbell, 1996. 83.

(5) Eihei Dogen. *Treasury of the True Dharma Eye, Zen Master Dogen's Shobo Genzo Vol. 1.* Ed. Trans. Kazuaki Tanahashi. Boston: Shambhala, 2010. 298-302.

(6) Okumura, Shohaku. *Lectures on 10th Chapter of Shobogenzo: Daigo (Great Realization).* Audio CD's from November 2008 Genzo-e. Sanshin Zen Community, Bloomington.

(7) Ibid.

(8) Okumura, Shohaku. *10th Chapter of Shobogenzo: Daigo,* Unpublished.

(9) Eihei Dogen: *Jijuyu Zanmai, Self-fullfillment Samadhi.* Clouds in Water Zen Center Chant book.

(10) Nishijima and Cross, Book 2, 106.

(11) Okumura. *Daigo,* Audio CD.

(12) Okumura, Shohaku. *Realizing Genjokoan: The Key to Dogen's Shobogenzo.* Boston: Wisdom, 2010. 81-87.

(13) Ibid., 86.

(14) Katagiri, Dainin. *Returning to Silence, Zen Practice in Daily Life.* Boston: Shambhala, 1988. 44.

(15) Okumura. *Realizing Genjokoan,* 87.

(16) Ibid., 81.

(17) Ibid., 86.

(18) Brown, Dan. *Lectures on Mahamudra.* Retreat at Mount Madonna Center, Watsonville, CA. February 2012.

(19) Tanahashi. *Shobo Genzo,* 297.

(20) Nishijima and Cross, 84.

(21) Okumura. *Daigo,* Audio CD.

(22) Tanahashi. *Shobo Genzo,* 297.

(23) Katagiri, Dainin. *Each Moment is the Universe, Zen and the Way of Being Time.* Boston: Shambhala, 2007.

(24) Joshu Jushin. *The Recorded Sayings of Zen Master Joshu.* Trans. James Green. Boston: Shambhala, 1998, Case 93, 39.

(25) Eihei Dogen. *Fukanzazengi, Universally Recommended Instructions for Zazen.* Clouds in Water Zen Center Chant book.

(26) Okumura. *Daigo,* Unpublished.

(27) Ibid.

(28) Ibid.

(29) Ibid.

(30) Ibid.

(31) Katagiri. *Returning to Silence,* 172.

(32) Okumura. *Daigo* Audio CD.

(33) Okumura. *Daigo,* Unpublished.

(34) Ibid.

(35) Okumura. *Daigo,* Audio CD.

(36) Ibid.

(37) Okumura. *Daigo,* Unpublished.

(38) Ibid.

(39) Nishijima and Cross, 89.

(40) Okumura. *Daigo,* Unpublished.

POLISHING A TILE, ACTUALIZING A MIRROR

Zazenshin

Josho Pat Phelan

Introduction

Soto Zen is considered to have begun in Japan in 1227 when the monk, Eihei Dogen, returned after almost four years of training in China. A characteristic of Soto Zen teaching is the idea that we are already enlightened or awakened, and, through practice, we realize or actualize this awakened quality of being. Therefore, practice is the expression or activity of the awakened heart and mind. As a young person, Dogen Zenji struggled with the question, "If all people are endowed with Buddha Nature, as the sutras teach, why is it that we have to train so strenuously to realize that Buddha Nature?" His insight into the answer to this question can be found in his radical teaching of the non-duality of practice and realization.

I will discuss the well-known story of "Ma-Tsu Polishing a Tile" from Dogen's teaching fascicles, *Zazenshin* and *Kokyo,* to show that, for Dogen, practice was not a means to attain enlightenment, but the manifestation of enlightenment inherent in all beings. When we practice zazen or Zen meditation to get something – a wonderful state of mind or quality – that we think we do not already have, that is delusion. By reaching out for it, we reach away from our inherent wisdom. In *Zen Mind, Beginner's Mind* Shunryu Suzuki (hereafter, Suzuki Roshi) wrote, "To take this posture itself is the purpose of our practice. When you have this posture, you have the right state of mind, so there is no need to try to attain some special state" (1). "Just remain on your cushion without expecting anything. Then eventually, you will resume your own true nature. That is to say, your own true nature resumes itself" (2).

Enlightenment is Inherent

In the 7th century, before Soto Zen (Ts'ao-Tung Ch'an) became a separate tradition in China, the Sixth Ancestor, Hui Neng taught in the *Platform Sutra:*

> ...the *Wisdom of Enlightenment is inherent in every one of us. It is because of the delusion under which our mind works that we fail to realize it ourselves....You should know that so far as Buddha nature is concerned, there is no difference between an enlightened man and an ignorant one. What makes the difference is that one realises it, while one is ignorant of it.* (3)

According to Dogen, the inherent wisdom within beings does not increase or improve with practice, nor is it diminished by our ignorance or lack of practice. Rather, practice is how we authenticate inherent wisdom, making it authentic in our lives. In his teaching essay "Buddha Nature" or *Bussho*, Dogen wrote, "Shakyamuni Buddha said, 'Living beings all are buddha nature.' ....Know that the *are* of *all are buddha nature* is beyond are and are not....The words *all are* are not limited to embryonic beings, original beings, inconceivable beings, or any other kind of beings. *All are* are free from mind, object, essence, or aspects. This being so, the body, mind, and environs of *Living beings all are* [buddha nature] are not limited to the increasing power of action, imaginary causation, things as they are, or the practice realization of miraculous powers" (4).

The idea that we are buddha nature or awakened is one of the fundamental teachings in Soto Zen. Suzuki Roshi said "...to be a human being is to be a Buddha. Buddha nature is just another name for human nature, our true human nature" (5). The word 'Buddha' means an awakened one, one who is awake to things as they really are without the coloring and attachments of our individual conditioning and karma. So another meaning of Buddha is unconditioned nature.

Unconditioned Nature

I think most of us are drawn to practice Zen meditation, or zazen, out of a sense that something is missing from our lives. We may feel a lot of stress or tension and want to become calm. We may have a bad habit, like smoking, that we want to stop, and we think that zazen may give us the support we need. Or we may come to practice out of mental or emotional pain or frustration. I would be suspicious if someone told me they had a strong conviction that they were Buddha, and they wanted to begin practicing zazen in order to realize their "Buddhaness." From our human point of view, most of us are motivated to practice out of pain or a deep need to change our lives. But, from Buddha's point of view, we are already Buddha, and when we practice, we are just expressing our awakened quality of being. We have unconditioned nature, or we *are* unconditioned nature; but at the same time, most of us are ignorant of our unconditioned being. Our habits and conditioning hang like a cloud covering our unconditioned nature.

One characteristic of conditioned nature is the feeling that there is something that we don't have that we need. From the time we are born, the way we are treated, the things we are told, and the way our language and society are constructed all support the notion that there is something that we don't have that we need. Whether we think we need new clothes, or a new car, or happiness, or fulfillment, or peace of mind, or even realization, whenever we feel that there is something that we need that we do not already have, we are ignoring our inherent completeness and setting up a duality between who we are and who we want to be. Trying to obtain something outside ourselves, which we think will make our lives better, is a form of dualistic grasping which can never be satisfied. There will always be something newer or something better available.

Because we are inherently awake, I don't want to suggest that we should just lie back and enjoy it. We need to take care of ourselves, to support ourselves, and to take care of our lives, and, as much as possible, take care of the environment and help improve living conditions for all people. But the Buddhist attitude is that we take care of our activity, and we take care of the world as our selves, rather than taking care of it as some "thing" out there that we are trying to help or improve. The Buddhist attitude is like the attitude you have when you change your baby's diapers. When you take care of your baby, you are not doing it to try to fix it—it isn't broken. Likewise, when we wash dishes or clean house, we don't do it because there is something "the matter" with these things. We clean house because that is how we complete the activity of living in a house or eating off dishes: the process includes cleaning.

In order to actualize the Buddha we already are, or to complete the activity of being Buddha, we need to practice. In the book, *Shikantaza*, there are instructions called "On Practicing Throughout the Day," written in the 14th century, that were given to laymen when they visited Zen monasteries. The instructions suggest that the way to practice throughout the day is to throw oneself completely into each activity. When you do zazen, do nothing else but zazen; do not think about enlightenment, do not think about Buddhist teaching. When you go to service, hold the sutra card with two hands and chant wholeheartedly; do not think about the meaning of the sutras, do not think about zazen. When you go to breakfast, fully attend to the food in front of you and realize the mind of eating; and when you rest, just rest. So when you sit zazen, just do zazen, and when you work, just work. In Soto Zen, this spirit of just sitting or just working, doing whatever it is you are doing with your whole body and mind, is common to all our activity. In this way wherever we are, whatever we are doing we have the opportunity to practice (6).

We don't have to be in the meditation hall to practice. Our practice is not even dependent on meditation. Since we are already Buddha, we can never leave the environment of practice. Soto Zen goes a step further and teaches that it is not even "we" who practice; rather, it is the Buddha we are who practices. Suzuki Roshi said, "Then eventually you will resume your own true nature. That is to say, your own true nature resumes itself" (7).

Practice-Enlightenment

I would like to continue examining the theme of inherent enlightenment, in which practice is viewed as the activity of inherent wisdom, rather than a means to cultivate enlightenment, by looking at Dogen's version of an exchange that took place between one of the Sixth Ancestor's disciples, Huai-jang, and his disciple, Ma-Tsu or Baso. Dogen discussed this exchange in his fascicles *Zazenshin* and *Kokyo.* Dogen introduced the story saying that it took place after Ma-Tsu had "intimately received the mind seal," or received Dharma Transmission from Huai-jang, indicating that Ma-Tsu was a mature practitioner when the story took place. In earlier versions of the story, Ma-Tsu is presented as one of many monks in Huai-jang's monastery. More than once, Dogen took a traditional text or story and reworded it to illustrate a particular point that he wanted to make. Chinese koans are fluid and can be used as examples of different aspects of practice, much like poetry can make more than one point or have more than one dimension. Presenting Ma-Tsu as a mature practitioner who had been practicing with Huai-jang for many years when this exchange took place, supported Dogen's view of the inseparability of practice and enlightenment.

At the time the story took place, Ma-Tsu was dedicating himself to the practice of zazen when one day Huai-jang came to Ma-Tsu's hermitage while Ma-Tsu was sitting in meditation and asked him, "What do you seek by doing zazen?" Ma-Tsu said, "I'm seeking to become a buddha [or I'm trying to get enlightened]." (Why else would he be sitting zazen all day?) So Huai-jang took a tile that had fallen off the roof and began to rub it on a stone in front of the hermitage, imitating Ma-Tsu's activity. He used the act of rubbing or polishing to represent the cultivation or refining of practice. After awhile, Ma-Tsu asked, "Master, what are you doing?" referring to the essential meaning of Huai-jang's activity. Huai-jang replied, "I'm polishing this tile to make it into a mirror." The mirror is a metaphor for enlightenment, or the still, reflective quality of the mind when it's free of discursive thought, when it simply reflects things as they are. Ma-Tsu then asked, "How can you make a mirror by polishing a tile?" Huai-jang replied: "How can you make a Buddha by sitting in meditation?" Ma-Tsu asked, "Then, what shall I do?" Huai-jang responded, "When you are driving a cart, if the cart doesn't go, should you beat the cart or beat the ox?" The cart is usually considered a metaphor for the body and the ox refers to volition or the mind. This reflects the Buddhist teaching that the mind is the source of our experience, and that all physical and verbal action is preceded by a mental impulse, a very brief thought or intention to act. Later, in *Zazenshin*, Dogen commented that he recommended beating the cart (8). Dogen took the traditional Buddhist teaching that the mind is the source of our experience, that the mind itself is Buddha, and turned it around by teaching that the Way is attained through the body.

Ma-Tsu did not reply and Huai-jang continued,

Are you practicing sitting meditation, or are you practicing sitting Buddhahood? If you are practicing sitting meditation, meditation is not sitting or lying down. If you are practicing sitting Buddhahood, "Buddha" is not a fixed form. In the midst of transitory things, one should neither grasp nor reject. If you keep the Buddha seated, this is killing the Buddha, if you cling to the form of sitting, you're not reaching its principle.

At this point, Ma-Tsu experienced realization, and, in both accounts of the story, he continued practicing with Huai-jang for ten more years, gradually deepening his understanding.

No Fixed Form

The story ends with Huai-jang's point that crossing your legs and sitting still, or taking the posture of a buddha, does not make you into a buddha anymore than polishing a tile will make it into a mirror. A buddha has no fixed form and practice has no fixed principle or method. Enlightenment is directly realizing the nature of mind, not just holding still. It is not something we gradually develop over time by refining our zazen practice, nor is our practice limited to what happens when we cross our legs. If you leave your practice behind when you stand up after zazen, you are dividing your experience into practice and non-practice.

We tend to do this, to compartmentalize our lives: my work is over here and I need to bring my effort to it; and this is my practice, so I need to be aware and present during this time; and someplace there is a little space for fun where I can just relax and forget about effort and awareness. When we do this, the result will be picking and choosing, developing preferences based on attachment to what we enjoy in practice and aversion to what we don't. This is the way we create and uphold discrimination in our everyday lives. Our human tendency is to bring this into our practice: "I like sitting zazen, but I don't like chanting," or "I don't like bowing," or "I don't like the *oryoki* meal (the monastic meal form)."

This exchange between Huai-jang and Ma-Tsu criticized the systematic practice or cultivation which occurred in some Buddhist traditions in which the practitioner might first take precepts to purify his unwholesome karmic patterns, and then cultivate compassion to strengthen his intention to practice for the benefit of all beings, and then practice with simple concentration exercises, working up to more complex methods that deepen concentration, slowly perfecting his meditation and developing insight through study, so that gradually he was ready for enlightenment. Instead, this story is supporting the notion of sudden enlightenment, that enlightenment or realization occurs instantaneously by seeing directly into the inherent wisdom of mind, which is the commonly accepted understanding of the story.

However, Dogen rewrote the dialogue, giving it a different emphasis in which he included both the activity of practicing with dedication over many years, as well as immediate realization, which is not dependent upon cause and effect. In doing this, he turned the traditional meaning of this story upside down. According to Dogen, the meaning of Huai-jang's question, "What do you seek by doing zazen?" could be expressed more accurately when it was read as the statement: "Zazen is that seeking which is the Absolute." In his teachings, Dogen emphasized the non-duality between zazen practice and realization. Because Soto Zen teaching begins with the premise that we are already enlightened, that we are inherently Buddha, it is actually the Buddha we already are that enables us to practice in the first place. When we practice it is the Buddha we are meeting Buddha. According to Dogen, realization is both inseparable from practice and an embodiment of ultimate reality.

Dogen expressed Ma-Tsu's response, "I seek to become a Buddha" as "Seeking is Buddha-actualization," and he commented on this by saying, "...zazen is always that 'buddha-actualization' which is one with 'seeking'; zazen is always that 'seeking' which is none other than 'Buddha-actualization.'" He also said, "Seeking is *before* and *after* (italics mine) Buddha-actualization; it is likewise at the very moment of Buddha-actualization" (9). In this sense, the first period of zazen we sit, the zazen we do after years of practice, and our zazen during a long *sesshin* (five- or seven-day meditation intensive), are all zazen. Each time we totally engage in just sitting, we practice absolutely; and absolutely means completely, totally, with an all-inclusive quality. So there is nothing left over or left out of our zazen. At each point in time, our zazen is Buddha-actualization, and there is no progress because there is nothing outside that moment of total engagement to compare it to. For Dogen, zazen practice and actualization were not separate.

Concerning the part of the story when Huai-jang was polishing the tile and Ma-Tsu asked, "What are you doing?" Dogen commented that "Polishing a tile has been present in the Absolute," meaning that the non-dual activity of Absolute reality is "tile polishing" or practice, and this "tile polishing never ceases." Nishijima and Cross translate this line as "The doing of what is always the polishing of a tile" (10). Sometimes Dogen used interrogatives including "how" and "what" to indicate Suchness or ultimate truth. According to Dogen, practice is how we express ultimate truth or the Absolute. "Absolute" does not mean that there is something that exists in an absolute sense. Absolute means the non-dual nature of reality; our inability to recognize this is delusion, the illusion that we exist separately from everything else.

However, in *Zazenshin*, Dogen went on to say that "tile polishing" or practice, as the natural expression of awakened nature, is not "mirror-making." This means that zazen is not something we do in order to produce the result of enlightenment. To practice zazen now in order to become enlightened at some future point is setting up a goal, something to attain that is separate from who we are right now. Dogen taught that practice and realization are simultaneous, that there is no realization outside our moment-by-moment practice.

Total Engagement

"Tile polishing," or our practice, is total, complete and self-sufficient. Therefore, one who is really engaged in zazen does not anticipate something down the line called enlightenment. If we do zazen now, thinking about some future enlightenment, we are not doing zazen. We are thinking about the future. In this practice, there isn't room for anything else, no room for future, no room for enlightenment, no room for Buddha, or insight. There is only room for one activity: total engagement in immobile sitting, instant after instant, and total, non-dual engagement is itself realization. There isn't room for the two activities of total engagement and realization. Total engagement *is* realization – total engagement is the activity of throwing our whole body and mind into our present activity without looking to the future for a result. Our practice, our very presence, is unique and non-repeatable, and each moment of being is complete just as it is.

After Dogen said that "tile polishing" (our practice) is not "mirror-making" (a technique that produces enlightenment), he went on to say that, "Unless we understand that all mirrors are products of 'tile polishing,' there are no buddha-ancestors' expressions, there are no buddha-ancestors' discourses...." When Huai-jang asked, "How can you become a Buddha by doing

Soon silence will have passed into
Jean dry   legend.

zazen?" it is traditionally seen as disparaging zazen practice. Dogen turned this around by saying "...one who practices zazen does not anticipate becoming a buddha. The practice of zazen has absolute significance in itself...practicing zazen is Buddha-actualization."

In *Dogen's Manuals of Zen Meditation*, Carl Bielefeldt wrote, "...zazen is not merely a utilitarian device producing a perfected state of enlightenment, but the expression of a more fundamental perfection inherent in all things. In this way, the practice of zazen itself becomes the actualization of ultimate truth, and the practitioner, just as he is, becomes the embodiment of perfect enlightenment" (11).

Dogen taught that practice is the way we manifest inherent enlightenment, not how one is transformed into a Buddha. Consequently, the tile does not become the mirror, because the tile already is the mirror. If you are practicing zazen in order to get something, some wonderful state of mind, or quality, that you think that you do not already have, that is delusion. By reaching out for it, you are reaching away from your own inherent completeness. As Suzuki Roshi said, "When you have this posture, you have the right state of mind, so there is no need to try to attain some special state. When you try to attain something, your mind starts to wander somewhere else. When you do not try to attain anything, you have your own body and mind right here" (12).

In the dialogue, Huai-jang said, "If you are practicing sitting meditation, meditation is not sitting or lying down. If you are practicing sitting Buddhahood, 'Buddha' is not a fixed form." Dogen expressed this as "If you cling to the sitting form, you cannot penetrate [the sitting-buddha's] principle." Then he made a leap and reversed direction by saying, "This 'clinging to the sitting form' means to abandon the sitting form, while enacting the sitting form. The truth is that once you sit as a sitting-buddha, it is impossible not to 'attend to the sitting form.' Because it is impossible not to 'attend to the sitting form,' 'attending to the sitting form' is,...'penetrating completely [the sitting-buddha's] principle.' This is what is called the dropping off of the body-mind" (13).

Dogen's way of practice is to just sit, without expecting anything, totally engaging body, mind, and this moment, as it arises instant after instant. Total engagement is realization. Because of this, realization is the practice of non-dual effort, not the result or accumulation of earlier practice. Dogen expressed this in his poem *Zazenshin* when he wrote, "Realization, beyond real or apparent, is effort without desire" (14).

Endnotes

(1)   Suzuki, Shunryu. *Zen Mind, Beginner's Mind.* New York & Tokyo: Weatherhill, 1976. 26.

(2)   Ibid., 49.

(3)   Hui Neng. *The Sutra of Hui Neng.* Trans. Mou-lam Wong. Berkeley, CA: Shambhala, 1969. 25.

(4)   Eihei Dogen. *Treasury of the True Dharma Eye, Zen Master Dogen's Shobo Genzo.* Ed. Trans. Kazuaki Tanahashi. Boston: Shambhala, 2010. Vol. 1, 234-5.

(5)   Suzuki. *Zen Mind,* 48.

(6)   Sokei Diachi. "Junji-hogo." *Shikantaza.* Ed. and Trans., Shohaku Okumura. Kyoto, Japan: Kyoto Soto-Zen Center, 1985. Reprinted in 2002 as *Soto Zen.*

(7)   Suzuki. *Zen Mind,* 49.

(8)   Bielefeldt, Carl. *Dogen's Manuals of Zen Meditation.* Berkeley, Los Angeles, London: University of California Press, 1988. 144.

(9)   Kim, Hee-Jin. *Flowers of Emptiness, Selections from Dogen's Shobogenzo,* Lewiston, NY: The Edwin Mellen Press, 1985. 155-165.

(10)   Eihei Dogen. *Master Dogen's Shobogenzo.* Trans. Gudo Nishijima and Chodo Cross, London: Windbell Publications, 1996. Book 2, 91-106.

(11)   Bielefeldt. *Dogen's Manuals,* 140.

(12)   Suzuki. *Zen Mind,* 26, 27.

(13)   Kim, *Flowers of Emptiness,* 161.

(14)   Eihei Dogen. *Beyond Thinking, A Guide to Zen Meditation.* Ed. and Trans. Kazuaki Tanahashi. Boston: Shambhala, 2004.

THE TRUE HUMAN BODY

Shinjingakudo

Shosan Victoria Austin

Body and Mind Study of the Way

In Buddhist practice, what is it that we are practicing? And how does the practice we set for ourselves, comprise a study of the Way? Soto Zen Buddhism emphasizes deportment, embodying dignity through bearing and ritual gesture. Each component of body and mind expresses attention, deep intention and remembrance of our tradition. For example, bowing at the end of a chant one morning, I noticed how complete our gestures are. A *gassho* (1) is such a concise practice device with which to directly experience body and mind as a crucial, ever-available means of awakening.

As we intend to *gassho*, all sorts of extra mental activity might come up besides the intention to bow, and the bow itself. We might face distracting thoughts or physical input. We might struggle to muster the energetic resources to bow at all, let alone correctly. We might be questioning our intention, performance, or relationship with the object or subject of the bow.

Traditionally in the Soto School, *gassho* is taught with the fingertips held a fist's width in front of the nose tip. However, the strict form can include a global experience of doing and discernment at many levels of body or mind. Physically, from a position of balance, the whole torso and both arms must perform one coordinated action. We touch the base of the palms evenly at the level of the base of the neck, the energy center of expression. This contact is the foundation for the mirror relationship between the fingertips and the tip of the nose. *Gassho* expresses non-duality – not one, not two. Constantly falling out of balance and constantly renewed, the even pressure of the palms asserts "Nondual!" immediately, directly, in a language that both body and mind thoroughly understand.

"The Buddha way cannot be attained unless you practice, and without study it remains remote." These words come from Dogen Zenji's direct teachings on "Body-and-Mind Study of the Way" to the assembly at his temple, Koshohorinji, in 1242 (2). In this fascicle, Dogen first emphasizes that body practice – *shugyo* – is how we attain realization. In fact, "[practice and realization] cannot be defiled" (3). Together, inseparably, they evoke the whole truth of the Way. Dogen teaches body and mind practice separately "for the time being." In other words, they are one within practice and realization (4). He proceeds to evoke the mood and gist of first how to study with the mind, and then with the body. Reflecting a holistic view of practice-realization, Dogen presents possibilities of mind to study directly: Buddha-mind (5), everyday mind (6), and skillful mind (7). Then, reflecting his devotion to the transmission of the Way, he shows how the practice lineage, including one's self, manifests the true human body that includes whatever arises.

Body-and-mind study of the Way awakens all three minds. For example, one morning as my *jiko* (8) and I bowed to each other, I noticed that he was lowering his *rakusu* (9) as he bowed. Traditionally, our form is maintain the level of the hands holding the *rakusu* at chest height as the torso bows. However, though I repeated my correction with every *gassho*, he would lower it each time. As I searched in my mind for a new way to correct him, I got inspired. I said, "What if you relax and decentralize your mind, so it rests in both places (10) at the same time?" He bowed correctly.

What mind gave the successful instruction, and what mind received it? Practice-realization can be seen as a moment of possibility. My *jiko* and I simultaneously let go of our mental pattern and discovered the traditional form anew.

Buddha-mind cannot be expressed in limited words, or grasped by the thinking mind. However, letting go creates a studious mind that actively transcends our limits.

Everyday mind is part of the bow as well. Contact between hands is earthy. Two people meet and greet. Skillful mind is in the bow, voiced by a teacher's learning from the lack of success of her previous instructions. The moment a teacher's instruction connects, the teacher's and student's experience mirror and touch each other. This is just like the teacher's own instruction from her teacher, and so on, back to Buddha.

The importance of *gassho* is not in the arcane detail. By placing the hands correctly, we study body-and-mind in the manner of the ancient sages, thoroughly refreshed and new. This is what is meant by "body-and-mind study of the Way."

Like all light-filled endeavors, such study is not without a shadow. Any bias we carry towards body, mind, or both, renders our understanding and expression, partial, divided, or sick. For instance, as a product of a mainstream Judeo-Christian American upbringing, I grew up with a deeply held preconception that body and mind are separate. Body was matter, and mind was immaterial and light. Mind could be spiritual and smart, whereas body was clay-bound and dark. This bias was so thoroughly established in my own body and mind that it was invisible to me. Body-mind separation partialized my self.

I did not perceive this rift, this suppression. If anyone had asked me, intellectually I would have agreed with the statement, "Body and mind are one." But until I had studied both yoga and Zen for many years, I carried and even practiced my childhood bias in ways unknown to me. Body and mind were *not* one, though I thought, and projected, that they were. My meditation practice tended to express "mind over matter," psychologically overriding physical pain. Though my form was physically correct, it was not integrated.

The mind-over-matter bias which marked my first steps on the Way may have been conditioned by a larger, and at the time, largely unremarked phenomenon: the social realities of who defined the practice-realization of the Way. All of my first teachers were male.

The purpose of this discussion is to comment on *Shinjingakudo*, not to argue feminism. Yet what study of body-and-mind that includes conventional reality, can be without gender? And what shadow does the majority male transmission (11) in our lineage throw on our practice of body-and-mind? Though Buddha meant his teaching for all human beings equally, to what extent could an all-male teaching group fully and precisely instruct a female body-and-mind? What shadows might thus be present both in Dogen Zenji's writing on body-and-mind, and on Western practitioners' interpretation and study of his teachings?

In her 2009 book *Zen Women: Beyond Tea Ladies, Iron Maidens and Macho Masters,* Grace Jill Schireson points to several areas of transmission and practice long devalued in our tradition that may take on new meaning in a climate of gender equality. Reverend Schireson includes sections on family practice and ties, sexuality, intimacy with vulnerability, feelings and emotions, work, and issues of aging. She notes that mother images including *prajnaparamita,* Perfect Wisdom, have been present in Buddhist literature and teaching for many years. However, body-and-mind practice and transmission has not acknowledged women's forms and physical realities. Such images are relatively new to the forms of Zen (12).

Although I mainly agree with Reverend Schireson, when I examine body-and-mind practice and transmission, I do find images, symbols and practices that call to the feminine in me. I would agree that the above psychosocial areas are indeed undervalued and need more attention. However, the main gap I personally experience, is psychophysical.

Many of the traditional meditation instructions on posture work well in general for male bodies, but not for female bodies. The 51% of people whose pelvis and spine are shaped one way thus receive instructions for the 49% of people whose pelvis and spine are shaped another way. Women's bodies are not usually mirrored by the traditional teachings. For instance, the common instruction, "Push the lower back slightly in," is likely to create an upright spine for a male pelvis with a high center of gravity; but for a female pelvis with a low center of gravity, this instruction creates anteversion. Many otherwise useful instructions that sharpen the effort of male body-and-mind, are far more likely to create imbalance in menstruating, pregnant, or menopausal body-and-mind.

After many years of conversations with Zen teachers and students, I believe that intellectually the American Zen tradition agrees with Dogen Zenji's teachings, at least in spirit. Body and mind are taught as one, in books and lectures throughout the land. Yet in practice, the mind-body split so central to the Western unconscious hides our deep gender bias in body-and-mind study. Though Buddha's teaching of how to relieve suffering is universal, as his descendants, our embodiment of that teaching is limited. Our assumptions about difference circumscribe how we physically, psychologically and intellectually respond to the world of variety: as suffering, or as the end to suffering. We more easily perceive one end or another of any duality we can name: body and mind, male and female, black and white, and so on.

So studying the assumption hidden in our unconsciously gendered responses to suffering, might shed new light on what Dogen might have meant by the "true human body." If we practice with such assumptions as body-and-mind, we can respond to infinite variety of the universe, with boundless practice.

Studying with the mind

Studying with the mind is the cultivation of awakening. This study is shaped by our intention to relieve human suffering. Each generation learns mind study by personal transmission from teacher to student. Mind to mind transmission can be seen as the vertical dimension of the Way – the generational hierarchy of teachers and students from Buddha to the present day.

Shinjingakudo reflects the mindset of Dogen's own awakening and transmission, here reported by his Dharma great-grandson, Keizan Zenji:

> *Once, during late night zazen, Rujing [Dogen's teacher] told the monks, 'Studying Zen is the dropping off of body and mind.' Hearing this, the master was suddenly greatly awakened. He went at once to the abbot's room and burned incense. Rujing asked him, 'Why are you burning incense?' The master answered, 'Body and mind have dropped off.' Rujing said, 'Body and mind have dropped off, the dropped-off body and mind.' The master said, 'This is a temporary ability; you must not approve me without reason.' Rujing replied, 'I am not approving you without reason.' The master asked, 'Why are you not approving me without reason?' Rujing said, 'You dropped off body and mind.' The master bowed. Rujing said, 'You have dropped off dropping off.'* (13)

Later, Dogen described the encounter as part of the vertical dimension of Zen practice: "I was able to enact this face-to-face transmission by dropping away body and mind, and I have established this transmission in Japan" (14). "This face skin is the great round mirror of all buddhas. Because they have the great round mirror as their face skin, they are unmarred inside and outside.

A great round mirror transmits to a great round mirror" (15, 16).

At first, the vertical dimension of practice means mirroring the practice of one's teacher, which in turn mirrors the ancient sages. When stability in this practice matures, one sees into this path and lineage transmission. The student's mind begins to reflect the Buddha mind as exemplified by the teacher. One realizes that it is none other than unbroken awakened mind, equal in everyone and everything.

This is the ideal. However, when we examine mind realistically, we see that our shadow keeps us from reflecting everything equally. Due to our assumptions and habits of thought, our mind develops "fault lines" that crisscross the mind. Mind takes on a specific, limited structure that seems broken, not unbroken. Yet we don't easily see our preconceptions. They are difficult to find and even more difficult to see through, like dense shadows. Let's take as our example how the preconception of maleness in our lineage might pre-structure and limit our great mirror of mind-to-mind transmission, until we find where it exists, and then see through it.

Though women and men are all human, with similar capacity for awakening, scientifically speaking, our brains are structured differently (17). Two such differences are 1) relationality, and 2) sensitivity and acceptance of pain and dissonance. For the first, the "importance and centrality of relationships in women's lives," as well as the implication of this centrality in women's lives, have been well documented (18). Second, our modern conventional view based on research is that between the two genders, the very perception of pain is different (19). To over-simplify, women tend to feel their pain more, and divulge this more to others, than do men.

When I first arrived at San Francisco Zen Center in 1975, the institution was culturally male. After Shunryu Suzuki Roshi decided to allow men and women to practice together, women gradually developed as practitioners, as teachers and as leaders. During crisis times, these women stepped in to lead the institution, resolve the crisis, and to create a new management style. Female leadership was instrumental in changing the institution from a "person-church" identified with a single leader, to a religious corporation led by many. Perhaps in the next several hundred years, the physical and physiological differences of the new female leaders will produce further cultural change – in social organization as well as in practice.

One example of possible change as a result of men and women's practicing together is in the strategies we use to handle dissonance and pain. Women's experience and valuing of relationship allow us to become pregnant with perceived conflict, rather than to reject it. We gestate and bring forth approaches that embrace inclusion. In conflict, a person with a relational approach tends to take sides less often than a person with a linear approach. Instead, relational people nourish and value the various concerns embedded in a conflict. Relational people mirror the concerns until a mutually beneficial solution can be found. This is a gender-based talent, a female talent: one organization's data sample showed the settlement rates of female mediators to be 20% higher than males (20).

This is not any special Buddhist quality of "enlightenment" – it is women's ordinary experience. Relational practitioners easily see and respond to different people's way-seeking mind (21). Could it be that relational practitioners embody the same talent within body-mind as well? For example, what does a relational person do when faced with the apparent contradiction between the need to sit still, and the pain arising in her knees? In a practice culture based on sitting still through the experience of pain, how might this difference play out?

My experience is that the advice given to students is often geared towards stillness and silence, with a strong dash of stoicism. What mindset might hold a heightened experience of pain and dissonance in a relational – a more female-body-minded – way?

The story of generational transmission of the Buddha-Dharma in Soto Zen, so far, is often unquestioningly accepted as the story of a line of men. In this story, the vertical, hierarchical dimension is reflected and mythologized in the institution of ordination and authorization. Until very recently, the official story was that men held the *Shobogenzo*, the treasury of the true Dharma eye, and that women did not. What does the maleness of the transmission imply about the mind-set of the tradition towards dissonance and pain?

In fact – contradicting the commonly accepted story – the historical transmission includes many women. However, the teaching lineages of these women have traditionally been interrupted or forgotten. One example is the suppression of the followers of Mahapajapati (22). Another example is the name of Prajnatara, the teacher of Bodhidharma, whom members of the Soto Zen Buddhist Association now think may have been a woman (2011), but who has been traditionally remembered as male.

This means that the generational transmission to women often includes a shadow transmission – namelessness, suppression, or non-acknowledgement. Our very bodies have been remembered as male. Our students have been dispersed from generation to generation, and our lines are only now being re-established.

Thus, the story of Buddhist women teachers – the mind-to-mind transmission story – includes the following fact. In a lineage that overtly studies peace and the relief of suffering, there is a strong covert history of oppression. This fact, this shadow in the mirror of transmission of Buddhism, has an impact on both men and women. Men, overtly in the light, suffer from a history of privilege. Women, covertly in the dark, suffer from a history of invisibility. For women, to study the Way with mind means to accept, layer upon layer, the shadow of the transmission. Along with acknowledgement as a teacher, can easily come a mind structure shaped by history. It is easy to carry forward the possibility that our style of transmission can be cut off, both in our own minds and in those of our descendants.

Let's look at the same issues, relationality and pain, to see how our mindset as practitioners might be limited by this shadow. A female leader recounted to me how her collaborative style was culturally devalued within the institutions of Zen. In fact, collaboration is part of this teacher's transmission of Buddhism, with strong ties to Buddha's teaching of interdependence. A student coached by this teacher might find himself or herself applying the teachings of interdependence to new situations by studying everyone's viewpoint equally, including that of a marginalized person or group. Yet this approach might seem slow or ineffective to those with a bias towards a more direct leadership style. Also, this teacher's Dharma style might have a tendency towards invisibility. The next generation might not hear about her valuable teachings, or pass them on.

And what about those with double invisibility? A disabled student spoke about how much persistence it took for her to follow the morning schedule. The residence requirement to follow the schedule completely was difficult or impossible for her, if she listened to her body and took things slowly in the morning. Though this practitioner struggled valiantly, the hierarchy felt that her difficulty in attending morning zazen made her unsuitable for temple residency. However, listening to the body and seeing as it was, was an important part of her Dharma practice. In the future, if this person becomes a teacher, the study of sitting with constructive pain rather than damaging pain will be an important contribution of her life and teachings.

We need to look at the possibility that the maleness of our transmission may have skewed our teachings and practices of studying the mind. Isn't it short sighted to assume that all minds will behave like male minds, in relation to pain, dissonance and suffering? Might relational and pain-acknowledging approaches be invisible or absent? Might some women be inclined to take on male assumptions about the nature of awakened mind? Wouldn't this be devaluing their own experience, which is actually their dharma?

A person who practices in the shadow must develop deep strength and unconditional confidence in the mind of awakening, to be able to continue without discouragement, depression or aggression. To my knowledge, this difficult experience of practicing in the shadow is only now beginning to be understood and included as a major element of training (23).

In the phenomena we call way-seeking mind, there is no male or female. Ultimate reality transcends gender differences or any other dualities. Way-seeking mind is the same in everyone. Can we accept this? Can we appreciate Buddha-mind equally, can we fulfill everyday activity in a way that manifests way-seeking mind, and can we develop the skill to relieve suffering, both in the light and in the dark? Can we study the mind so holistically that we truly understand its oneness?

Studying with the body

Studying with the body means progressively developing the direct experience of awakeness through physical form. Due to the material, easily seen aspect of form, studying with the body (at least in my experience) lends itself easily to the expression of the horizontal or non-hierarchical aspect of the Way. Every being is embodied, and every part of the body has a part to play in the meditation we call "studying with the body."

Speaking of *shikantaza,* or the direct experience of reality while counting breaths in sitting, Suzuki Roshi said:

> The counting—if you—it looks like different from—counting-breathing practice looks like different from the shinkantaza. But actually, if you, you know, practice it, [there is] not much difference. Because purpose of counting-breathing practice is not, you know, to count. No, it is quite easy to count your breathing, you know, if you try to count, just count.
>
> Why it is difficult is—you have to—you have to have right posture, and you have to make—and all parts of your body should participate in the practice of counting breathing. And your mind should follow the counting, and your arm, and mudra, and legs, and spines, and, you know, muscles should join—participate [in] the counting-breathing practice. And it is more than concentration to—it is more than to be concentrated on your counting. Concentration usually means mental practice, you know, but counting-breathing practice is not just a mental practice but also

physical practice too. Then (there is) not much difference between shikantaza and counting-breathing practice. (24)

Why would Suzuki Roshi teach that the deep experience of *shikantaza* is similar to breath-counting practices that any beginner can do? Suzuki Roshi's Dharma ancestor, Dogen-zenji, explains as he introduces the process of studying with the body:

> *To study the way with the body means to study the way with your own body. It is the study of the way using this lump of red flesh. The body comes forth from the study of the way. Everything which comes forth from the study of the way is the true human body.* (25)

Thus, every moment of posture adjustment, silent awareness of the body, or breath counting is a process of acknowledging and verifying the body, the whole body.

Although conventionally we use the word "body" to denote our physical form, demarcated from the rest of the universe by the boundary of our skin, we also use the word "body" to denote many forms. For instance, we speak of a body of truth, a body of knowledge, a governing body, an organic body, or a Golgi body (part of a cell). Dogen is saying that all these bodies, when thoroughly studied, comprise the true human body.

So at first, the study of the body might seem so infinitely varied as to be disparate or confusing. Within the body, suffering may arise at any level from the cell to the social body in which a practitioner takes part. Suzuki Roshi often spoke of "things as they are" – which I think refers to such experience of the body. "Things as they are" can be contrasted with another term of Suzuki Roshi's, "things as it is." Once, early in my practice, when I asked a senior student what Suzuki Roshi might have meant by these two terms, he responded that he thought the difference in the two terms came from Suzuki Roshi's unfamiliarity with English. Now I believe that the difference in terms is deliberate – that "things as it is" refers to studying with the mind, and "things as they are" to the horizontal aspect of studying the variety of the body at its many levels.

In my experience, when we study the body through the body, our initial confusion develops into a systematic discernment of parts of the body, types of pain, the four great elements, postures, breathing, the social aspects of practice, and the forms and choreography of ritual – in other words, an apprenticeship in the variety of embodiment, both internally and externally. Difference matures into discernment. Discernment matures into a direct appreciation of any physical form as an expression of suchness.

Studying with the body allows us to discover a deep appreciation of how we, and all beings, "come thus" (26). When we truly appreciate the suchness of things as they are, we understand how one thing exists with another – hand-to-hand, side-by-side, in mutual transmission of Buddha nature, appearing and responding freely, awakening everyone and everything.

With respect to gender, it might be useful to understand how physical and physiological differences between men and women might play out in the discernment of suchness.

Specifically, what is it to awaken in the body of a man, and what is it to awaken in the body of a woman? A generalization of gender-specific phenomena might help us understand some of the practice norms we encounter in studying with the body.

In a man, a high center of gravity and the capacity for large-muscle strength, plus high reserves of oxygen, give our hypothetical practitioner a talent for what I call "sprint strength." He is able to take on a physical challenge; he recovers quickly and is ready for more. Because a man has a relatively narrow, tall pelvic girdle, often slightly tipped back, with strong muscular support at the outer hips, the meditation instruction, "push your lower back slightly forward," will produce a feeling of alertness. And because he physically thrives on competition and challenge, he may experience "interdependence" as relatively unknown, and the experience of relationship as a vast step into a great mystery.

In contrast, our generalized woman practitioner is someone who has experienced menarche, menstruation, and perhaps pregnancy and menopause. She has faced blood and profound change as regular occurrences in her life, whether or not she and her practice environment acknowledge this. Her center of gravity is lower; her pelvis is wider and often slightly tipped forward. An instruction to "raise the front of the spine" would make physical sense for her. Her physical strengths are endurance, fine muscle control, relatively wide peripheral vision, and good eye-hand coordination. She has relatively greater lower body flexibility, but also a tendency towards lower body tweaks and injuries. Because she is physiologically geared towards cooperation, she may experience individuality as relatively unknown, and the experience of asserting her awakening as a vast step in the study of the Self.

Returning to the experience of *gassho* with which we started, we can understand that our hypothetical, generalized male and female practitioners might experience practice and awakening in very different ways. They both place their hands together in front of the face. However, the similarity could end there. Their path to the direct discernment of the true human body in *gas-sho* may take greatly different psychophysical forms.

Let's look at what happens in the body in *sesshin*, an extended meditation retreat, over seven days. Through the power of concentration, many experienced practitioners, whether male or female, have the capacity to flood pain signals with bliss. In this discussion, let's assume that they are studying the body and have not used concentration to override pain.

Our hypothetical man did not find it easy, as a beginner to cross his legs. After months or years of practice, his muscles and ligaments are loosening up. He wants to learn how to sit in full lotus, so he crosses his legs and pulls his feet close to his torso, ignoring a slight pain in the knees. In the first day, he finds that his body settles down, but the knee pain becomes worse. By the third day, though the pain is present, if he changes postures occasionally, he can handle it. On the sixth night, he decides to sit up all night to emulate the Buddha's effort, so he does. Strong, effortful sitting turns effortless sometime during the night. He reports an experience of clarity and peace. On the seventh day, sleepy but settled, overall he concludes that he has come closer to his goal of sitting in full lotus through a whole *sesshin*.

Our hypothetical woman was able to draw her legs into full lotus after a few months or years of practice, but now, her hip hurts. The pain in her knee and hips gives her a feeling of unsteadiness and doubt. She decides to study how her knees and hips function. However, on the second day she begins to get cramps, and by the third day her menses have arrived. Now all her joints ache, distracting her from the question of knees and hips. By the sixth day, her flow is over, but her physiological state has changed in the process. She is stiffer than on the first day, though more concentrated. To save her knees and hips, she alternates between crossing her legs, and kneeling. She doubts whether the schedule is physically good for her, and studies other people to see whether they seem to be in pain. On the whole, she cannot decide whether to go to the night sitting. Maybe not. By the end of *sesshin*, she feels pretty good about the way she has learned to take care of herself. Underneath it all is a growing feeling of concentration and confidence in Bodhi-mind. But the next day she feels hung over and cranky. She is left wondering about *sesshin* as a physical practice, and resolves to discuss this with her teacher and other participants.

Both the man's body and the woman's body are capable of sitting still. However, as in their process of studying the mind, their study of the body may take quite different routes. As previously discussed, this man's practice may be more effectively mirrored by the lineage teachings. This woman's practice may be seen as resistant or lacking resolve. However, a good teacher will see and respond to the student's own study of the body. He or she will listen to the student's words and offer guidance on how to settle "the body in the body," as Buddha taught (27).

No matter where a student begins, it is possible to cultivate the experience of awakening in the body. The forms of practice are designed to provide this experience. For instance, when beginners use *oryoki* (28), just opening the bowls, receiving food, eating, and putting the bowls away requires major effort. Studying the body occurs at a gross level. For experienced students, studying the body with *oryoki* form might include mindfulness of which finger opens the knot, or how one's own deportment in chanting affects the energy of the room. Movements become more refined, not through goal-oriented drill, but by the intimate study of all levels and layers of the body within strict forms. There is a progressive development of awakening through form.

Body-mind study of the Way leads to wisdom

Let's return to the question with which we began this exploration. In Buddhist practice, what is it that we are practicing, when body-and-mind unite? And how does the practice we set for ourselves, comprise body-and-mind study of the Way?

Although as gendered beings we may take apparently different paths homeward, at rock bottom, we are all human beings with similar issues. The nature of human life gives rise to suffering, unless we are awake. We practice and study the uniting of body and mind, and through each practice we awaken, thus coming to the transcendent relief of suffering. In body-mind study we taste what is permanent, wholesome and truly ours, beyond the impermanence, illness and anomie of the life of suffering. We experience freedom.

Here is how Dogen summarizes body-mind study of the Way:

Zen Master Yuanwu said, 'Birth is undivided activity. Death is undivided activity. Filling up the great empty sky, straightforward mind is always bits and pieces.' You should quietly pursue and examine these words. Although Zen Master Yuanwu once said this, he did not understand that birth-and-death further overflows undivided activity... With birth and death as its head and tail, the entire world of the ten directions, the true human body, freely turns the body and flaps the brain. When turning the body and flapping the brain, it is the size of a penny, it is inside a particle of dust. It is the vast flat earth, it is a sheer eight-thousand-foot cliff. Where there is a sheer eight-thousand-foot cliff, there is the vast flat earth. In this way the true human body is manifested as the Southern and Northern continents. To examine this is the study of the Way.

The true human body is the bones and marrow of the realm beyond consciousness and unconsciousness. Just raising this up is the study of the way. (29)

In all the forms that transmit the presence of awakening, whether handed down from the ancients or discerned from the many beings, we mature our body and mind. We cultivate the united body-mind until it is wide enough to hold any concept of difference, and deep enough to endure throughout time.

At the bottom, at the base, at the ground of any of these forms, there isn't anything permanent that we can find. If a human being thoroughly examines the human body-and-mind, he or she observes that it is subject to change, and that it eventually dies. It doesn't stay gendered, injured, or even limited by the skin as it did before such study. We clearly observe that this changeability is part of the miracle of conditioned existence, part of the miracle of life. This body, with all of its limitations and all of its talents, with all of its needs, inconveniences, and joys, is the body of awakening. We can experience our life coming forth in accord with the fully-experienced body and mind of all beings, of all time and of all space. This is the study of the Way.

Acknowledgements

I would like to express gratitude to Rev. Zenkei Blanche Hartman, Rev. Myoan Grace Jill Schireson, Rev. Surei Darlene Cohen, and Camilla Dickinson for conversations that helped develop my thoughts about Shinjingakudo and gender issues in the transmission of the Dharma. I offer boundless gratitude to my twin, muse and editor Jacqueline Austin, without whose help this article would not have been possible.

Endnotes

(1) Gassho: Hold the palms and fingers of both hands together. Your arms should be slightly away from your chest, your elbows should extend outward from your sides in a straight line parallel with the floor. The tips of your fingers should be approximately the same level as your nose. This is an expression of respect, faith and devotion. Because the two hands (duality) are joined together, it expresses "One Mind." "Definition of Gassho" in SOTOZEN.NET http://www.global.sotozen-net.or.jp/eng/practice/zazen/manners/index.html. Website page. (Soto Zen website, "Manners").

(2) Eihei Dogen. "Body-and-Mind Study of the Way." *Moon in a Dewdrop: Writings of Zen Master Dogen.* Ed. Trans. Kazuaki Tanahashi. San Francisco: North Point Press, 1985. Section 1, 87.

(3) Ibid., 87.

(4) Ibid., Section 2, 87.

(5) The mind of ultimate reality; awakened mind.

(6) Mind as we usually experience it; conventional experience and reality.

(7) Experience of the one, or ultimate mind, in its many forms.

(8) Incense attendant.

(9) Small Buddhist robe modeled on the *okesa* ordination robe.

(10) Torso and hands (I pointed).

(11) How Buddha's teachings are passed from master to disciple, generation to generation.

(12) Schireson, Grace Jill. *Zen Women: Beyond Tea-Ladies, Iron Maidens and Macho Masters.* Somerville: Wisdom, 2009.

(13) Keizan Jokin. *The Record of Transmitting the Light: Zen Master Keizan's Denkoroku.* Trans. Francis H. Cook. Los Angeles: Center Publications, 1991. 227.

(14) Tanahashi, 181.

(15) A great round mirror, reflecting everything equally, symbolizes Buddha-mind.

(16) Tanahashi, 1978.

(17) Many studies support this assertion, including 2012 contributions such as "Intrinsic brain activity differs between genders: a resting-state fMRI study in a large cohort of young healthy subjects"; the TRAILS study; sex differences in relation to pain and tobacco smoking cravings; in moods during episodes of tinnitus; all available through PubMed.

(18) See Covington and Surry, "The Relational Model of Women's Psychological Development: Implications for Substance Abuse" for a brief survey of recent models of women's psychological development.

(19) "Women Feel More Pain than Men, Research Shows" – see www.sciencedaily.com, www.medicinenet.com, and many other public sites.

(20) The Center for Legal Solutions, Inc. Marietta, Georgia, 2008. Web page.

(21) *Bodhicitta*, or awakening mind.

(22) Walters, Jonathan S. "Gotami's Story." In: *Buddhism in Practice*. Ed. Donald Lopez. Princeton: Princeton University Press, 1995. 113-138.

(23) Buddhists in several countries speak about the need for such practices to transcend suffering based on the shadow of difference in many areas: race, gender, ability, and so on, in the late 20th century up to the present day (Reported by Soto Zen Buddhists). Soto Zen Buddhist Association, Listserv, 2011. Unpublished e-mails.

(24) Suzuki, Shunryu. Lecture. Tassajara, August 18th, 1969. Unpublished transcript.

(25) Tanahashi, 91.

(26) "Thus Come One" is an epithet that expresses the Buddha's physical manifestation in the world.

(27) See any translation of the Mahasatipatthana Sutta, section 1, "Mindfulness of the Body."

(28) "Just Enough," the bowls used in formal Soto Zen meal ceremony in the meditation hall.

(29) Tanahashi, 94.

ON THE MOON AS ONE'S EXCELLENT NATURE

Tsuki

Eido Frances Carney

When we engage in dialogue with the ancients, we bring them fully into life in this moment. We give them voice when we take up their teachings and we dwell in their company in conversation on the mountain. Because we practice Dogen's Zen teachings, he reverberates continually in our experience and has enough volume to answer our questions. He is an active presence in our practice just as Shakyamuni Buddha is in the Enlightenment of all sentient beings. We don't so much *study* Dogen as we *practice* Dogen. He is a spiritual giant who shines light on a Way so that Buddha Nature can be realized and expressed.

Dogen dwells in the Absolute, relentlessly prodding us to apply ourselves immediately and resolutely to the great matter of life and death. What he seems to do, for me, is to steer me into a linguistic shower that begins to soak into the veins the more I am able to sit with him and allow his language to be the very river flow of Dharma. Dogen believed that language itself was the tool to open and liberate us, and thus as a linguist he had the ability to play with language poetically, to nudge the mind beyond the intellect so as to soak in the very water that reflects the moon in order to move us to the experience of Awakening.

Hee-Jin Kim says, "Enlightenment, from Dogen's perspective, consists of clarifying and penetrating one's muddled discriminative thought in and through our language to attain clarity, depth, and precision in the discriminative thought itself. This is enlightenment or vision" (1, 2). Kim points out that the liberating quality of Dogen's language was meant to open the way of the Bodhisattva to use language skillfully to relieve suffering in the world, to make the inexpressible, expressible (3).

In the title of the fascicle *Tsuki*, in *Shobogenzo*, (all quotes from *Tsuki* are italicized) Dogen employs the Chinese characters that mean "one's excellent nature" and renders them as "moon" in the Japanese. So, while the word *tsuki* may mean simply the word "moon," he doesn't mean an object floating in the night sky, but rather here in the title it infers much more. Dogen invites the moon as Buddha Nature, Buddha Mind, One's Excellent Nature, One's Original Nature, and the moon, which reflects all of existence.

Later in the fascicle, Dogen does use the simple character *getsu* to mean the concrete moon, but it isn't always clear whether he is referring to just the concrete or whether he is suggesting Buddha Nature. We are asked to allow Dogen's words to stream in us so that the meaning floats up into awareness such that a wider world becomes evident. We are asked to be intimate with Dogen, bathing in the moon-reflected water where we enter with him the Mind of Buddha Nature. When we read Dogen, it helps to remember that we cannot rest on one concrete meaning, as we are often inclined to in the English language. He strings his metaphors together touching lightly here and there as if he were forming a road map or a web. And indeed he is; he is tracing out a route. Kim also says that language points to the specific and it also liberates. So Dogen constructs and deconstructs in a single blow. He moves us out of our restive place into a new dynamic that causes us to probe, wonder and weigh the dilemmas in the unities of opposites. Dogen moves between three characteristics of the manifested world, which are separate and yet are simultaneously one: we are *like* Buddha Nature, we *are* Buddha Nature, we *reflect* Buddha Nature (4). To use one is to infer all three.

We might question what we mean by Buddha Nature. This is not something that we can immediately comprehend or arrest by definition. The teaching of Buddha Nature comes in Shakyamuni Buddha's discourse in *The Lotus Sutra* in which the actual nature of the Buddha is transcendent which means that all beings participate in the Realization of Buddhahood. The Buddha tells us that "All sentient beings *have* Buddha Nature through and through." Dogen translates this teaching as saying, "That which we have through and through *is* Buddha Nature" (5). This means that it is not something to acquire, not something we can attain, and not something we can possess. Rather it means that we are inseparable from Buddha Nature, that we are thoroughly Buddha Nature itself. The activity of life is Buddha Nature. The moment-by-moment manifestation of life is Buddha Nature. Buddha Nature is itself life and the activities of existence, the circumstances we come to, the action of compassion that is *now*.

In another fascicle *Bussho*, On Buddha Nature, and throughout his teachings, Dogen continually invents new ways to express Buddha Nature as a pivot point of understanding that comes through a direct experience of impermanence. "What is impermanent is, of course, Buddha Nature," says the Sixth Patriarch (6). Dogen goes on to say, "The physical presence of a Buddha is someone's manifesting the Spiritual Body, and Buddha Nature exists as that person's manifestation of the Spiritual Body" (7). In other words, life in its apparent form is itself the spiritual body, and Buddha Nature is its essential manifestation of that body. "Not a single moment, not a single thing exists that is not with life; not a single event, not a single mind exists that is not with life," writes Dogen (8). This means that all of life is a unifying dynamic, in motion, whose activity is Buddha Nature. There is nothing other than life making effort into and as life. This comprises all of existence and "both the self and the world share their common destiny as the self-activities and self-expressions of Buddha nature" (9). The leaf in its fall through autumn air is Buddha Nature. Water being water as a waterfall is Buddha Nature. Soup cooking on the stove is Buddha Nature.

Although *Tsuki* is a brief fascicle, Dogen delivers various facets of teachings using the metaphor of the moon as Buddha Nature. He explores the concrete nature of existence, the phases of the moon, which cannot be measured in our usual way of time. Our own Buddha Nature is manifesting differently from moment to moment and yet it is also the whole of Buddha Nature.

As Dogen's teachings are completely practical, that is, praxis distinguished from theory, or something that we actually do, they must be completely practical if they are to remain alive. If Dogen's teachings had not been practiced for many centuries, they would not have lived but would have become an artifact. The very fact that Dogen's Way was put into practice from the very beginning is demonstration of this. The writings were not the emphasis, the practice was. There are three wisdom teachings from Dogen that appear in this fascicle that give us tools toward active praxis and spiritual movement in our lives. These are: the nature of space as practice; swallowing as complete digestion and comprehension of Buddha Nature; and, vomiting it out (which might include the slight action of spitting) as manifesting practice as the way of actualizing Buddha Nature in this world, this life, this existence here and now.

The Nature of Space as Practice

Dogen begins *Tsuki* with a teaching on the nature of space. He starts with a little poem by the Buddha:

> *The true Dharma Body of the Buddha*
> *is unbounded like empty space.*
> *It reveals Its form by conforming to an object*
> *like water reflecting the moon.* (10)

The real Dharma Body of the Buddha is just like unbounded space. One of the qualities of the Buddha is spaciousness. Wherever Shakyamuni Buddha went, a sense of spaciousness was created around him, and his followers could sense a vast and safe continuous openness. This universal quality remains in our experience and is ever present but becomes palpable in the intimacy of Buddha Nature. As we continue in the practice of Zazen, we begin to realize space as a quality of being, a way in which we dwell with all of existence allowing the world, all phenomena to be as it is. Dogen says that all phenomena is simply Space! He says:

> *The real Dharma Body of the Buddha is just like unbounded space. And because this 'unbounded space' is the Real Dharma Body of the Buddha, the whole earth, the whole of all realms, all thoughts and things– that is all things that manifest—are, in themselves, unbounded space. The hundreds of things that sprout up and the myriad forms that they take—all of which manifest before our very eyes—are just like the Dharma Body of the Buddha, and they are the real Dharma Body of the Buddha, and they are like the moon in water.*" (11)

Notice Dogen's use of "is just like," "is," "are just like," "are in themselves," "are just like," and "are." He's encompassing everything and showing that to speak of the Moon, or to speak of Space either as itself or as metaphor is to mean the concrete, the image, the experience and the idea as a single Reality.

Dogen refers to a koan in another fascicle called *Koku*, Space:

> *Zen Master Shakyo Ezo of Bushu asks Zen Master Seido Chizo, "Do you understand how to grasp space?"*
> *Seido says, "I understand how to grasp it!."*
> *The Master says, "How do you grasp it?"*
> *Seido clutches at space with his hand.*
> *The Master says, "You do not understand how to grasp space!"*
> *Seido says, "Well, how do you grasp it, brother?"*
> *The Master grabs Seido's nostrils and he pulls on them.*

Seido is groaning with pain and he says, "It's very brutal to yank a person's nostrils! But I have directly been able to get free."

The Master says, "Directly grabbing hold like this, you should have got it from the beginning!" (12)

When the Master grabs Seido's nostrils he's saying "You are the space that space is grasping!" We ourselves are unbounded space and what we think is concrete and substantial is just space, the insubstantial Buddha Nature being exercised, utilized, expressed, unfolded in life.

We have no central continuing self, we have no unchanging self, we are continuously changing and all of existence is continuously changing. We are floating in a realm of existence in form, in visible, physical form as space. This is the crux of Buddha Nature to be alive in the reality of continuous life experience as space. It must be shown that Dogen does not exclude the nature of being/time in his notions of space, they are intertwined and inseparable, but in the *Tsuki* fascicle, he does not dwell on the metaphysics of time/being. As I've said, *Tsuki* is a brief chapter that stays close to the promise of its title. The Moon is the referent point.

Still, the adventure of exploration into practice that Dogen continually invites means that we see "space" also as "Emptiness" since the Japanese character for space also infers Emptiness. The Master is also saying to Seido, "You are *MU*. You are Emptiness itself, completely manifesting moment by nostril-pulling moment. Pulling the nose is the *MU* of the nose as *MU*. Pulling the nose is Buddha Nature. Pulling the nose is Space. Space is the nose." Dogen is again using language in a way that opens, expands, invites, and refuses to arrest any dynamic in one unfermented concoction.

One discussion will also include another. If he discusses space as space, we may experience what he is after, but if we haven't, we will have a chance to get it in his discussion of "Emptiness." He provides numerous angles and ways of seeing.

Dogen offers space as the first dynamic of the Moon. Shakyamuni Buddha and Dogen Zenji were practical people in that they gave us a praxis that we could use, not just something to put on the shelf, such as a book. All of the teachings are implements that we can pick up and swallow and use. Taking the notion of space, really practicing with it, walking through daily life day by day understanding, "Oh, this is space," looking at each person and understanding, "This person is space just as I am." Dogen means we treat everything as empty space. Treat everything and everyone as a deliberate practice of space saying, "Oh here is space, space dwelling in space." If I shake someone's hand, this is the same as moving through her, like grasping Seido's nose, as becoming two impressions or presences merging. This is not to give away our particularity; it is to understand what boundaries are necessary and what boundaries are not, or when to use boundaries and when to not use them. You are not me and I am not you, but you and I are intricately presupposed in the connectivity and atmosphere of space.

When Dogen's teachings are actually praxis and authentically applied, we rise above the tendency to create the activity of Buddha Nature as mere techniques to help us through the anxiety of living. Perhaps uncertainty has infected every society because of the existential nature of what it means to be alive. We imagine that if we can be rescued quickly, we can return to our usual comfort and continue unchanged and proceed without the inconvenience of too much inquiry. Techniques may have their place, but for the long run, they only cover up anxiety for a time until we search around for yet another technique. This may continue until we are simply a bundle of techniques, still in search of the Original Self. Being the discomfort of anxiety, searching out for ourselves what it means to experience ourselves as space, is Buddha Nature. Zazen is the mediator in this exploration, the space in which we dwell as the foundation of practice.

We can allow the world around us to be as it is and then we can see it, and gain some insight about how to assist, or how to help a particular situation. Because, we are space within space, this is Buddha Nature, this is the Moon; It is to be the Moon and Emptiness itself. This is to be the light of the moon, shining forth in all the aspects of our lives. *It reveals Its form by conforming to an object* (13). Does Dogen mean, and does Shakyamuni Buddha mean that we reveal our Buddha Nature by conforming to the shape of this body, like water reflecting the moon? Such as taking this form in order to reflect Buddha Nature? The only way we can express Buddha Nature is to be in form and in the activity of life, in being. If we are not in existence, Buddha Nature is not expressed. At the same time that we are form, we are unbounded space, in this existence. This is what we are!

At times Dogen uses the moon as a metaphor but he says that the moon that you can think of is also the real moon, and the metaphor is the Reality! So the moon reflected in water is the same as looking at the moon. Your reflection in someone's eyes is the same as looking at the Moon and that is our meeting place. To see another and see the Moon is seeing Buddha Nature. Buddha Nature reflects Buddha Nature. So we come together in our true meeting place in the reflection of Buddha Nature.

The Moon also is manifested in the nature of image making and idea. In his book, *Visions of Awakening Space and Time: Dogen and the Lotus Sutra,* Taigen Dan Leighton expounds on this notion. *The Lotus Sutra* is a highly imaginative, visionary tract that Dogen referred to in his teachings throughout his lifetime. Leighton says that, "Dogen used *The Lotus Sutra* especially to express his worldview of earth, space, and time themselves as awakening agents in the bodhisattva liberative project" (14). To further explain the importance of space and image, Leighton quotes David McMahan, "The ability of the visual system to apprehend vast areas, long distances, and many things simultaneously is often highlighted in Buddhist literature and associated with the sense of spaciousness....This sense of sight as capable of encompassing wide spaces and penetrating to the furthest depths of the cosmos is important to the development of the imagery of Mahayana sutras," and to our own ability to consult image as the unfolding enlightenment within us (15). Consider how this faculty of image and space-making plays out in humanity's scientific explorations of deep space science. We think about our own galaxy and we know other galaxies exist. So, the Hubble spacecraft was sent in search of content to be found in a dark point in the sky that is to us from planet Earth about the size of a pinhead. Frankly, the scientists expected only darkness. What they discovered, however, was the light of billions of galaxies – not just stars, but whole galaxies appearing in the camera! Infinite possibility of expression! Just space, space and more space, endless space, infinite space. If I close my eyes, and I look into deep space, and if I can just imagine all of that, that is who we are, that is us, limitless. This ability to sense vast areas of space is the activity of Buddha Nature. The globe, the earth we stand on, and where we reside is the Buddha's home, Dogen's home, and it is our home. This manifestation right here where we are breathing is the portion we must care for. Right here, right now is the responsibility of practice, the very same as Awakening into Space and limitlessness.

Swallowing as Practice

Dogen continues with a poem by Master Banzan Hoshaku:

> *The Moon of our heart and mind is solitary and at the full.*
> *Its light swallows up all forms that arise.*
> *Its light is not something that illumines concrete objects.*
> *And concrete objects, in turn, are not things that truly exist.*
> *When Its light and objects both vanish from sight,*
> *There is still That which is the What.* (16)

What is meant by "swallows up"? Earlier I said that there is Buddha Nature like empty space, there is swallowing It up, and then there is vomiting It out. And the swallowing It up means understanding and comprehending – completely comprehending in the same way that when we understand something, we really digest it, fully engage with it and bring it wholly into the body and mind. Swallowing It up means to be genuinely intimate with Buddha Nature.

The matter of physically swallowing is primal in us. Our lives depend upon swallowing. When we are dying, in those final hours we may be deprived of the ability to swallow. Someone, if we are lucky, will keep the mouth moist so that sores don't develop on our tongue. Even in dying we maintain the dignity of the body. In birth, our first necessary event is to swallow air. So the breath and swallowing are partners in the life of the body. The baby must swallow the mother's milk if it is to live. As we grow, think of all we will swallow in life! Food, air, joys, anxieties, fears, laughter, sorrows, friendships, misfortunes, indignities, wars, tsunamis, births, deaths, marriages, earthquakes, triumphs, betrayals, killings, rapes, fires, wind, teachings, dirt, dust, oil spills, chemicals, accomplishments, music, love making, healings, volcanic eruptions, disappointments, grief, and more grief. We will swallow our tears, swallow when we meet confrontation or experience loss.

We use the word "swallow" in referring to nature's profound activity. We might say that the volcano swallowed the village, the ocean swallowed the settlement and its people, the tide swallows the beach, the mist swallows the trees. Just as Dogen tells us that the whole earth is actually our true body, he uses language to draw us into the most complete imaginable activity. The totality of swallowing is its complete disappearance. Where does the past actually go? Where is the reality of the future? We simply swallow up and vomit out. The light of the Moon "swallows up all forms that arise." Buddha Nature swallows up Buddha Nature. This is the true activity of life.

When we have an image of something in the mind, everything is swallowed within us. Where else is it? When I see the image of the Buddha on the altar, Buddha is already swallowed, completely gobbled into me or into you. If we look at the moon, we have swallowed the moon, thus we can comprehend and fully understand the nature of space and ourselves as Buddha Nature. Swallowing up also means we have fully engaged in practice and comprehended the teachings of the Buddha. There is no end to the realization of Buddha Nature so swallowing up begins with whatever tiny drop of realization is swallowed. But, swallowing has nothing to do with a particular amount. Perhaps we get a little glimpse at this point as we keep questioning, looking into our lives, holding the sacred, and we get more and more glimpses, more and more openings, more and more facets of the light of the Moon, endlessly pointing the way and swallowing up. Each glimpse is its own totality and is a complete glimpse.

Master Hoshaku, in his poem says that "they (concrete objects) are not things that truly exist." He means there is no permanent inherent unchanging self. That is also what he means when he says "the phenomena don't exist"; he means things are forever changing. Everything swallows itself. Dogen explains further, *What is now being expressed is that without fail the Ancestors of the Buddha as disciples of the Buddha possess the Moon of their heart and mind, because they treat their Moon as their heart and mind* (17). So they possess Buddha Nature of the heart and mind and they treat Buddha Nature as their heart and mind. Dogen says, *If it were not the Moon, It would not be their heart and mind. And without a heart and mind there is no Moon, there is no Buddha Nature. Solitary and at the full means that it lacks for nothing* (18). Everything has been swallowed.

It is quite important this question of swallowing it up, of comprehending, fully understanding that It lacks nothing. All of our life-situations are implicated so this is not an esoteric matter, but a very real question of life. We throw ourselves into practice, and we know that there is some tremendous yearning that brings us to practice in the first place. We feel there is something absent in our lives, maybe we are suffering, maybe we come with this sense that if we don't make it here, we're not going to get it. Sometimes this practice is called the final practice, because we feel that our very lives are at stake. We know that there is something we need to

answer, something we have to do. We may feel strongly
that if we don't get the answer, we are going to die on the
cushion, but we can't live without finding the answer.
We are in an existential trap, an emotional insis-
tence, a great and important urgency. Where will we go
to address that? Thus we come to Zazen, because Zazen
is a space dwelling in space that accepts every aspect of
us. There is nothing that we can hide in Zazen, and
there is nothing to hide in Zazen. We come quite naked
in heart and mind to the practice of Zazen and address
serious life issues. That is also what we mean by "swallowing it whole."

We will never, ever completely comprehend Zazen
or the entirety of the meaning of Space. Dogen says few
people fathom what space is. He says, even the master
who grabbed the other master's nose and twisted it, he
didn't exactly get it either, because if he really had gotten it, he would have twisted his own nose (19). Further,
Dogen says, "...you should have understood how to
grab hold of your Fingertips with our fingertips....you
need to explore through your training with your Master
the ins and outs of Space. And you need to explore
through your training the killing off of "Space" and the
revitalizing of It, and you need to know the relative importance of 'space'" (20). We don't have to think we
will comprehend everything at once. Zazen admits ev-
erybody and there is no end to it just as there is no end
to life. Yet there is still that yearning to at least address
our own lives as "swallowing it whole"; in swallowing it
and being able to comprehend perhaps the intention
of our own lives and to once and for all meet even a
glimpse of the Original Self. This is a glimpse that allows us to settle into our lives, to understand what our
right path is, and how we can make our way along that
path, knowing we've had a glimpse of Buddha Nature.

Kobun Roshi said about this, "We don't come to practice in order to make ourselves a better person. We come to be who we truly are." Meaning we come to the activity and the practice-experience of Buddha Nature because that is who we truly are.

So this swallowing It, is wonderful in the notion that we would be able to swallow the Teachings, digest them and hold them in this Dharma Body, the whole Dharma Body of Sangha. This swallowing It and being able to comprehend what we can, and use it on behalf of our lives is remarkable and essential. We can see that there is just the manifestation of Buddha Nature. There is the prolific appearance of life, but this particular appearance, the life you and I have now in this particular body, is only one time.

Then the question rises: how do we swallow? Our lives require tremendous care, and those moments in which we might be given an insight, just a delicate tiny moment that might open us, is fragile and takes genuine effort, much commitment to practice on the cushion, to be present for that fragile moment. In our effort to realize a glimpse of our Buddha Nature somehow, we have to truly embrace the vow of the Bodhisattva over the long-term, and give effort to practice.

All kinds of thoughts come into the mind when we imagine what it would be like to clearly see Buddha Nature. As Dogen Zenji points out, in Genjokoan, "When someone has spiritually awakened, he resembles the moon's 'residing' in water: the moon does not get wet nor is the water shattered" (21). It doesn't rattle the water, it doesn't shift it, it doesn't change it. Seeing our Buddha Nature is like that. We don't throw away our responsibilities because of it nor do we turn into someone other than ourselves. Dogen says, *Whatever is going on right now in our daily life will be just some of the hundreds of things that sprout up in our mind ever so clearly within our Moon, and it will be what sprouts up in the minds of the Buddhas and Ancestors within their Moon* (22). There's no absolute answer, it's just that Awakening is most natural because Buddha Nature is the most natural way to be. It is what we are. Completely natural, like truly realizing the moment of coming home. So, swallowing the Dharma, being the Buddha Body, this is what Dogen Zenji is urging. Swallowing completely. *And being intimately acquainted with your self, through and through, is being intimately acquainted with your Moon through and through,* says Dogen (23).

Solitary and at the full means that it lacks for nothing. Coming to the realization of Buddha Mind, to Buddha Nature, is understanding once and for all, we lack nothing. There is nothing else we have to be; there is nothing else we can be actually. This is it. There is nothing lacking in existence. We are spiritually incorrect when we think that we lack anything at all. It is an affront to the Dharma to think that we lack something. It is the same about any kind of claim that we make about existence. There is nothing missing (24). *A Buddha of the past once said, "The whole of your mind contains everything, and everything contains the whole of your mind"* (25). What could be missing? Swallowing the Dharma Teaching, swallowing the Buddha Body, comprehending, understanding, digesting the Buddha. This is the way of the heart and mind. This is the way of the Moon.

Manifesting Practice

How does Buddha Nature manifest? How do we actualize Buddha Nature? How do we vomit it out? To manifest or actualize means to make something real, actual, visible, demonstrated, apparent, evidential.

Dogen's poetic language refers to phases of the moon, sometimes it's full, sometimes it's dark, sometimes it's half full, depending upon its various phases.

Great Master Tosu Daido of Shushu Province, was once asked by a monk, "What is the Moon like when It is not yet full?"

The Master answered, "It swallows up three or four Moons."
The monk then asked, "And after It is full, what is It like?"
The Master replied, "It vomits out seven or eight Moons." (26)

This is the manifestation of realization as vomiting out seven or eight Moons, meaning that, Buddha Nature is manifested in the total expression and experience of our lives. Everyone finds a different expression. The word "vomiting out" asks, how is Buddha Nature spiritually expressed? We can say that this is the coming to the cushion for Zazen as the actualization, the manifestation of Buddha Nature.

What do we do with our lives when we get off the cushion? This is the great difficulty. We cannot languish on the cushion forever, we cannot hide in Zazen, yet Zazen is the profound Teaching that actually shows us how to live in all aspects of life. These aspects of practice are Buddha Nature in action. We engage in rituals, we chant, we ring the bells, we make offerings, we cook, we eat, we clean the temple, we study, we sew our robes. These Buddha Nature activities go on ceaselessly. At the same time that we say these expressions are Buddha Nature in action, there can be no "inaction" to Buddha Nature because Buddha Nature is all the activity of life.

Yet we ask the question: How do we actualize? For lay practitioners this may be a more pressing question than it is for a monastic whose life is circumscribed within the whole expression of Zen. But even Dogen did not try to answer this question except to say repeatedly, "Examine it for yourself." The point of the whole of his teachings is to show us a Way of Realization. It isn't something that we do just once; we actually do it every day, every moment. We sit Zazen, truly entering Space, truly being Space, swallowing completely in the practice of Zazen, and then when we get up we put Practice into practice. Swallowing and vomiting it out are one, as Buddha Nature manifesting in myriad ways, myriad forms.

We have this problem then of how to land and what route to take after we get off the cushion. This is the subject for our lives, and although we come to the cushion as the experience of our Original Self, our Buddha Nature, we still must climb underneath our existential dilemma: what shall I do with my life? How shall I live? Can I address my fears of living and dying? If we learn to really live, we learn to die. If we learn to die, we learn to live. These questions are completely informed by the practice of Zazen, by swallowing completely. It is the practice Dogen implores us to take. There is absolutely nothing to vomit if we don't swallow!

There is a very fine metaphor, which is called a *shul* that is a Tibetan word for an impression that is left by something that is no longer there (27). It's like seeing the indentation of our own chair or the zafu when we rise and walk away. That's a *shul*. And in the same way, the Ancestors and the Teachers who came before us have left a *shul* for us to follow so that we may see into our own Buddha Nature. These teachers are no longer there, but there is a path that we can follow, an impression of where their footsteps have been. That's a *shul*. Tendo Nyojo Daiosho, the Old Buddha of Mount Tendo said, "It is like Eka's coming over the snows to do his respectful bowing or like Eno's standing amidst the winnowed rice and doing his respectful bowing; these are excellent examples. They are the traces of former Ancestors. They are the Great Invocation" (28).

Carrying the metaphor a little farther, we ourselves are also a *shul* because we are empty of permanent characteristics, we are simply Buddha Nature, there is no permanent abiding self, so we are a collection of processes and sensory input, and mental formations, and that changes from moment to moment. Every single second, we are a different thing. So, we are just an impression of something that is no longer there. We mistake ourselves for a real person, but the actual pathway that is Space, that is Buddha Nature, keeps us centered as we walk. It allows us to ask: how do I manifest the Buddha Dharma, how do I manifest as Buddha Nature? We prepare for a ceremony, and we exert great effort in the evenings, training for the ceremony, and great effort at learning what we need to do. Then we do it! In this activity of practice we have created a *shul*. We did all the actions and it's no longer there, but it provides a path to follow. Dogen Zenji's life is a *shul*, a path to follow. He says, *One inch of the Moon's movement is equal to the full realization of the Tathagata, and the full realization of the Tathagata is but an inch of the Moon's movement* (29). In other words, we cannot measure either our activity or our essential nature. We but move in practice as easily as the Moon in its being is '*solitary and at the full.*' The Moon and its essential nature are one. In each moment we are creating a *shul* that has an effect on others around us, and everyone who comes into the Zendo leaves an impression for others to follow in the future: a path forward, a way to manifest Buddha Nature.

The Moon reflects the Sun, the Buddha, the sunlight. Just by shining It vomits. When we're looking at the moon we're actually looking at the sunlight. The light of the Moon is its vomiting forth. That's what the

Moon does. The Moon swallows everything. The Moon vomits it out. It teaches us this notion of phases that we are moving through, always changing and not always with the realized brilliant light of Buddha Nature and yet Buddha Nature is always there. The Moon holds the nature of Buddha Nature and sometimes it shines brilliantly, sometimes it's dark, and sometimes it's just a little light. Always changing, utterly free *with a swish of one's sleeves, taking one's leave to go to the Meditation Hall is what the Moon is* (30).

Endnotes

(1) Kim, Hee-Jin. *Dogen On Meditation And Thinking: A Reflection On His View Of Zen.* Albany, NY: SUNY, 2007. 63.

(2) For a more exhaustive study of Dogen on language see Hee-Jin Kim who pays particular attention to Dogen's logical and liberative use of language in both *Dogen on Meditation and Thinking* and in *Eihei Dogen, Mystical Realist.*

(3) Kim, Hee Jin. *Op. Cit.* 65.

(4) Eihei Dogen. *Shobogenzo.* Trans. Hubert Nearman. Mt. Shasta, CA: Shasta Abbey Press, 2007. *Tsuki* Footnote 2. 546.

(5) Eihei Dogen. *Bussho* 244-247.

(6) Ibid., 257.

(7) Ibid., 262.

(8) Eihei Dogen. *Zenki* 172.

(9) Kim, Hee-Jin. *Mystical Realist.* Boston: Wisdom Publications, 2004. 172.

(10) Eihei Dogen. *Tsuki* 545.

(11) Ibid., 545-546.

(12) Eihei Dogen. *Koku* 846.

(13) Eihei Dogen. *Tsuki* 545.

(14) Leighton, Taigen Dan. *Visions of Awakening Space and Time, Dogen and the Lotus Sutra.* NY: Oxford Univ. Press, 2007. 4.

(15) McMahan, David. *Empty Vision: Metaphor and Visionary Imagery in Mahayana Buddhism.* London: Routledge Curzon, 2002. In: Leighton, *Visions,* 101.

(16) Ibid., 546.

(17) Ibid., 547.

(18) Ibid., 547.

(19) Eihei Dogen. *Koku* 848.

(20) Ibid., 848.

(21) Eihei Dogen. *Genjokoan 33.*

(22) Eihei Dogen. *Tsuki* 548.

(23) Ibid., 548.

(24) For an exposition of the nature of Lack and its influence on our modern society, see Loy, David. *Lack and Transcendence: The Problem of Death and Life in Psychoanalysis, Existentialism, and Buddhism.* Amherst, NY: Humanity/Prometheus, 1996.

(25) Eihei Dogen. *Tsuki* 547.

(26) Ibid., 548.

(27) Batchelor, Stephen. *Buddhism Without Beliefs.* NY: Riverhead, 1997.

(28) Eihei Dogen. *Sesshin, Sessho* 544.

(29) Eihei Dogen. *Tsuki* 550.

(30) Ibid., 551.

ALL BEINGS SING THE SONG OF DHARMA

Mujo Seppo

Jisho Warner

The Song of Dharma

The dharma is a universal truth that is expressed in
uncountable particular ways. This one world of dharma
does not exist outside of all the individual manifestations,
and it is fully embodied in each one. Each and every thing
is the dharma world, and everything in its unwavering
activity of life expresses the dharma. How shall we know
this for ourselves, how shall we verify it? When we first
come to Zen we are offered a vision of what we are doing
as the practice of awakening to the reality of life. As we
practice, we test and digest this, and so we come, slowly,
to practice as awakening, and to practice as actualizing
the reality of life. At some point we have a sense of the

ongoing simultaneity of practice and realization. And that is the cornerstone of Eihei Dogen Zenji's teaching.

For a long time, I considered practice-realization to be something for people to do, at least those so fortunate as to be drawn to Soto Zen. What about all the other beings with whom we share this spinning blue Earth? In an inclusive universe, everything together makes up the dharma universe of dancing and glancing change that interweaves ceaselessly. We are all cousins, at the very least. No one, and no thing, is excluded, not even you or me on our worst days. It remains true whether or not we are aware of it.

Our practice depends on our personal initiative and energy, and yet that is only part of it. We are oriented and taught by the world around us, by what we don't yet know. The energies we call on for inquiry and action rise in us but don't originate in us as our own independent entities. In *Shoakumakusa* (Do Not Do Evil), Dogen said, *As you bring your body-mind to practice, . . . the four great elements and the five aspects of self of right now, of today, are practiced. The power of the four elements, the power of the five aspects of self that are the practice of right now—this power makes the four elements and five aspects be practice.*

Great energy is native to the four great elements of earth, air, fire, and water. It is equally native to our human selves, so often described by the five aspects of self *(skandhas:* form, feeling, perception, volition, and consciousness), which are of course made of the four elements. It is no different whether we think in terms of the four great elements or the hundred-plus elements of the periodic table. The basic elements interact energetically in all things, functioning with the power we call life, or ten-direction universe, or buddha, or dharma. Dogen says that all naturally practice; that is, all fulfill their nature completely. And he says that the power of this fulfilled nature is the basis of our practice; it is the motive power, the engine. *As this power makes even the mountains, rivers, earth, sun, moon and stars practice, so the mountains, rivers, earth, sun, moon, and stars in turn make us practice. . . . This is the living eye of all times and all places.* The endless pulse of life energy, the native power of life right now, makes practice happen as a natural function of life. This is true of all beings, not just humans. Rivers and stars are fully expressing the dharma of impermanence and interdependence. All beings naturally support each other's awakening practice as they sing the song of dharma.

The Sounds of Mountain Valleys

Dogen returned many times to the core themes he presented in his seminal early writings like *Bendowa* (The Wholehearted Investigation of the Way), *Fukanzazengi* (Instructions for Zazen), and *Genjokoan* (Actualizing the Fundamental Point), further examining what he had said. The dharma expressions of other beings, one of his principal ways of describing practice-realization, are first explored in *Bendowa*. He wrote in *Bendowa* that *all things come forth in awakening and practice all-inclusiveness.* All the many beings on Earth are actively expressing the dharma, which means that all are engaged in practice-realization.

The heart of *Bendowa* is the *jijuyu zanmai* (lit., "samadhi of the self receiving and employing") section, a glorious statement of the samadhi of the whole self endlessly giving and receiving. Everything he says in *Bendowa* about this samadhi is interleaved with statements about the dharma activity of beings other than humans. He says in a key passage, *Trees and grasses, walls and fences expound and exalt the dharma for the sake of ordinary people, sages, and all living beings. Ordinary people, sages, and all living beings in turn expound and exalt the dharma for the sake of trees, grasses, walls, and fences.* Their lives are inextricably linked to our samadhi: neither kind of being, and neither kind of practice, exists without the other.

The *Shobogenzo* (Treasury of the True Dharma Eye), Dogen's collection of essays, is full of such explorations. In *Dragon Song,* he opens our ears to the singing of dragons in withered trees. In *Valley Sounds, Mountain Colors* he examines the dharma singing of the buddha as it takes place in natural features of the landscape. The essay is built around a verse that the great Chinese poet Dongpo composed after an awakening experience one night, when he heard, in the stream burbling outside his window, the Buddha's broad tongue endlessly singing dharma.

Valley sounds are the long broad tongue.
Mountain colors are no other than the unconditioned body.
Eighty-four thousand verses are heard through the night.
What can I say about this in the future?

Dogen says these *voices of insentient beings speaking dharma are resounding even now, still blended with the sounds of the night's stream.*

In the *Mountains and Rivers Sutra* he quotes the Chinese master Furong, who said, *The green mountains are always walking.* Dogen comments that *mountains' walking is just like human walking . . . even though it does not look the same as human walking.* Moving, "walking," is an expression of life, and thus an expression of dharma, shared by the most diverse beings. We can learn about human walking by exploring mountains' walking, and about mountains by studying human movement.

In *Insentient Beings Speak Dharma*, also translated as *The Preaching of the Insentient*, he goes further into this grand vision of all things expressing the dharma. The many beings are not simply present in the dharma world in a perhaps passive inclusiveness. At all times they are manifesting the dharma through their life activities. Moreover, they are always speaking the truth of their nature. Master Furong didn't say the mountains sometimes walk, he said they are always walking. How could it be otherwise, when the dharma universe never stops? The word *preaching* in this title drives home the point that it is the dharma they are speaking, not just anything, as they constantly walk and sing: all beings are always singing the song of dharma.

The Speaking of the Insentient

Dogen opens *Insentient Beings Speak Dharma* with a profound and succinct statement. Then, in a pattern he often follows, he expands on what he has just said, the meanings spreading out like concentric ripples around a stone dropped in a pool. He says, *Speaking dharma by means of speaking dharma actualizes the fundamental point that buddha ancestors entrust to buddha ancestors. This speaking dharma is spoken by dharma.*

At the very outset, he puts us on notice that he is not concerned with the special activities of a subset of beings: *speaking dharma* actualizes the fundamental truth of dharma, and it is spoken *by dharma*, by what is common to all. *Speaking dharma* is a way for Dogen to describe the activity of practice. He is pointing to wholehearted body-and-mind engagement in life. He says that to do one's life fully is to express dharma completely. He puts his seal on this idea by saying that speaking dharma *actualizes the fundamental point*, which is to say the *genjokoan*.

Speaking dharma is a way to describe the actualization of each individual life, because speaking is something done by each one, it can never be a generalization. And yet, as he says, *speaking dharma is spoken by dharma*, not somehow independently invented by you or me.

In case we might like to think of ourselves as exemplary dharma speakers and to feel broad-minded when we stretch our minds to include hummingbirds and hemlock trees, Dogen pushes the gate open all the way: insentient beings are also speaking dharma, at all times, and *in this speaking dharma by insentient beings there are all buddhas, all ancestors.* The insentient speak the full and complete dharma.

Which beings are sentient and which are insentient? We make categories, like *conscious* and *unconscious,* and then we argue about where to draw a line between what is aware and feeling, and what is unaware and inanimate. Discriminating this way is a natural part of the human enterprise, but it gets us into terrible trouble, because we forget that all these divisions are delusory anthropocentric impositions on reality—sometimes refined tools, often stumbling blocks, never absolute truths. *Insentient beings speak dharma* means that wherever we draw a line between beings, that line is irrelevant to our deepest concerns. Opening the gate this way is the purpose of Dogen's emphasis on *insentient* beings.

Sentience is a combination of awareness and responsiveness. Certainly all living beings have some kind of awareness and are responsive to their environments. All have means to get their needs met and to promote their survival: all sense the way to lunch. Even single-celled creatures can be aware of light and move purposefully toward it; all can differentiate nourishment from waste. No living being can be truly said to lack awareness and responsiveness. This responsiveness means that all are living in reciprocity, giving and taking.

But what about *fences and walls, tiles and pebbles?* Dogen says in *Bendowa* that they all *carry out buddha work.* They are not alive, and they don't feel as we do, lacking nerve endings and tear ducts. But they are made of the same elements as living beings, and we are made of them: you and I are water, carbon, nitrogen, and a little cosmic dust. Certainly the non-living or non-sentient are responsive to their environments. Ocean waves erode stones into beach sand, while offshore boulders force incoming waves up into sprays of foam. Whatever we point to as insentient has a history, a present impact, and is part of the ongoing chain of consequences. All have reciprocal relationships: every door that opens or closes in front of us, every cloud passing overhead, is interacting with us in a mutual relationship.

I do not know how to evaluate the awareness of stones and mountains or how to make sense of them as subjects of their own being-ness. I cannot experience from their point of view. Rather than evaluate them, rather than say they do or don't have awareness, we'd best not impose our values and categorizing mind on them. That would both belittle them and limit what we can learn from them. How do any of us learn from them about life? By finding shared ground. And here it is: the insentient speak the dharma.

The Speaking Never Stops

In *Insentient Beings Speak Dharma,* Dogen presents a koan from Tang-dynasty Zen. *Master Huizhong was asked by a monk, "Do insentient beings understand dharma when it's spoken?"*

Huizhong replied, "Clearly, insentient beings always speak dharma. The speaking never stops.

This great declaration echoing down the centuries to us confirms that all beings are always speaking dharma, the insentient too. Master Huizhong reinforces this, or seals it, by saying that this speaking—even by the insentient—never stops. It is always happening. How can this be? As Dogen said in opening the essay, *This speaking dharma is spoken by dharma.* The dharma never stops, and it is never static or passive, it is always speaking, always expressing itself. *The speaking never stops.* This is life as endless movement and exchange, giving and receiving life and meaning ceaselessly.

The master is not answering the monk's question directly. The monk asked if the insentient have ears to hear with, and wit to understand what we might say to them. The master answered instead that the insentient are always speaking the dharma of buddhas, ancestors, and ordinary beings. The master is leaping beyond his student, who sees a beneficent human reaching down kindly to edify a lowly form of being. The master re-orients the monk: the insentient are not a passive recipient of our wisdom, but speakers of dharma truth in their own right.

We usually think of speaking as something that depends completely on conditions: body, mouth, air, tongue, mind, speaker, hearer. Dogen says no, dharma is spoken regardless of varying conditions and body parts. *Speaking dharma is neither sentient nor insentient. . . . It is not caused by creating or not creating. It doesn't depend on conditions.* This speaking is undivided and beginningless; it doesn't depend on conditions or leave any traces behind. Yet it is only particular voices, in particular circumstances that speak it, because phenomena are always particular.

Speaking dharma happens in myriad ways, in all kinds of actions, not only those that issue from throats. In just this way, all beings speak dharma, including insentient ones. *In this speaking dharma by insentient beings there are all buddhas, all ancestors.* The speaking of the insentient isn't limited by their conditions. There are conditions, and there is the dharma that is universal, that is not itself the limited conditions it is about. All buddhas are present throughout the universe, not picking and choosing.

Who Can Hear It?

The master's answer led the monk to a glimmer of the reciprocity that is the crux of understanding, so he persevered.

> *The monk asked, "How come I don't hear it?"*
> *Huizhong answered, "You don't hear it, but that doesn't mean others don't hear it."*
> *The monk asked further, "So tell me, who hears it?"*
> *Huizhong said, "All the sages do."*
> *The monk asked, "Do you hear it, master?"*
> *"No," Huizhong said, "I don't hear it."*
> *The monk persisted, puzzled, "If you don't hear it, how do you know that insentient beings understand the dharma?"*
> *Huizhong concluded, "This fortunate person doesn't hear it. If I did, I would be equal to all sages. Then you couldn't hear me expound dharma."*

Huizhong points out that the monk's inability to hear the dharma speaking of the insentient does not prevent others from hearing it. The speaking and hearing are everywhere and unceasing. The monk wonders about this *hearing* that he can't tune in to. The rest of the exchange is about who hears whom. Sages can hear sages, like hear like. *Sages* are those who are wise, those who, like Shakyamuni, the Sage of the Shakyas, are buddhas. It is not relevant to our quest to define the term closely; like *insentient*, it is a word for referring beyond definitions and boundaries.

It is fortunate for the monk that his master is an ordinary being like him, so that he can at least attempt to understand what his teacher says. It is fortunate for Huizhong, too, that he is an ordinary being, since he has dedicated his life to teaching ordinary beings. Sages' and insentient beings' ways of speaking are not our kind of language: how can we communicate truly? Dogen is clear that *just because insentient beings do not use the voice or the manner of sentient beings in speaking dharma, you should not suppose that the way insentient beings speak dharma is different from the way sentient beings speak dharma.* The insentient neither speak in a different kind of way, nor speak a different dharma.

The dialogue about hearing the insentient speaking dharma and what we can learn from them was taken up again about a hundred years later by the great Soto ancestor Dongshan and his teacher, Master Yunyan. Dogen relates their exchange this way.

> *Dongshan asked Yunyan, "Who can hear insentient beings speak dharma?"*
> *Yunyan said, "Insentient beings hear insentient beings speak dharma."*
> *Dongshan asked, "Do you hear it, teacher?"*
> *Yunyan said, "If I heard it, you could not hear me speak dharma."*
> *Dongshan answered, "Being so, I don't hear you speak dharma."*

> *Yunyan replied, "You haven't been hearing me speak dharma. How could you hear insentient beings speak dharma?"*

Dongshan is seeking a way through the thicket of the earlier koan. He picks up where the earlier monk left it: *who hears it?* Yunyan says that *insentient beings hear insentient beings,* that like communicate with like. This would seem to erect an insurmountable inter-species barrier—and how much greater the barrier between sentient and insentient.

Dogen cuts through this apparent barrier by reminding us that our ideas of who gets sorted into the *sentient* box and who into the *insentient* box are foolish at best, and that the boxes are not separate anyway: *In the assembly of beings, those who hear insentient beings speak dharma are insentient, whether they are sentient beings or insentient beings, ordinary or sacred.*

The Ears Never Hear It, Only the Eyes Do

Dongshan concluded his dialogue with Yunyan with a poem that opens a way to a true meeting. This is how we can hear:

> *How splendid! How wondrous!*
> *Inconceivable! Insentient beings speak dharma.*
> *The ears never hear it.*
> *Only the eyes do.*

Dongshan says we have to open up our doorways. This involves discerning, not in the service of analysis, but of experience and synthesis, discerning with body, heart, and mind engaged. In his time, *ears* often represented intellectual learning, and *eyes* intuitive understanding, the reverse of our modern view.

195

Commenting on Dongshan's poem, Dogen says, *Hearing dharma is not limited to ear sense and ear consciousness. You hear dharma with complete power, complete mind, complete body, and complete way, from before your parents were born.* Before your DNA was assembled, the way to your life was already opening up. The power or energy of life is always moving, and it is always us. Hearing dharma is not our personal accomplishment; it is the power of life operating.

He goes on to say, *You can hear dharma with body first and mind last. . . . Don't think that you are not benefited by hearing the dharma if it does not reach your mind consciousness.* This is true of us humans and also of all other beings: we benefit from hearing and speaking the dharma whether we know it consciously or not, and whether we have a human sort of mind-consciousness or not.

How does this work in our own experience? *Effacing mind, dropping body, you hear the dharma and see the result. With no mind and no body, you should hear the dharma.* In zazen we can directly experience this kind of hearing and speaking. Dropping off body and mind in just-sitting (*shikantaza*), we go beyond distinctions of sentient and insentient. Adopting the posture of awakening with the whole self, we speak dharma with our whole self (*ji-juyu zanmai*, the samadhi of the whole giving-and-receiving self).

When we sit zazen, we speak universal dharma in a human voice, beyond distinctions of eyes and ears. Because we are doing nothing else, we are speaking clearly, just as the so-called insentient are speaking with their clear voices. The dharma-speaking of zazen is beyond our comprehension. We "just" do it. Likewise the dharma-speaking of other beings is beyond our comprehension. We just—it's hard to put a name to it. We just respond, just sit together, just share the planet and the power of the four great elements.

Grasping with Your Body How All Sages Hear

Dongshan says *the ears never hear it.* Hearing and speaking dharma is too subtle a matter to leave to the intellect. The thinking mind absorbs and makes sense, but it also confuses itself in the effort. It fails to make sufficient sense of what is different from it, because its frame of reference is narrow.

The eyes hear it. We have to call on all our faculties. To learn truths from other beings, and to learn our own truths through those relationships, we have to use all our senses and body and feelings and intuition and mind. It is no help if we disparage the mind just because it cannot do everything and thinks it can.

The eyes that hear the dharma are the eyes on Kuanyin's thousand hands. The bodhisattva Cry Regarder (Avalokiteshvara, often in the feminine form of Kuanyin) perceives and takes in the cries of the world with an eye in every extended hand. Dogen expands on this: *There are eyes on a thousand hands, a thousand true dharma eyes . . . on ears, tongues, and minds. There are a thousand eyes throughout the body.*

The *thousand eyes throughout the body* were opened up to Zen practitioners in a famous dialogue between dharma brothers Yunyan and Daowu (Case 89 in The Blue Cliff Record).

Yunyan says, "I say that all over the body are hands and eyes."

Daowu answers, "Brother, you have only eighty per cent of it: Throughout the body are hands and eyes."

Every nerve ending and every cell is awake in its own way. All of life is reciprocity and awareness, giving and

197

responding. The Cry Regarder hears the dharma speaking of all beings, the suffering and the joyful voices, and responds appropriately, skillfully, to all.

There are eyes and ears on every oak leaf. There is a singing tongue and a hand on every twig. We notice colorful blossoms, so we think that's the flower's song. We get infatuated with shiny things, just like crows, but the bark and cambium and duff and stems and the mycorrhizal communities of roots and fungi are singing as subtly and as skillfully as the blue and purple blossoms. Throughout the body of the universe are hands and eyes. Ours included.

Letting Ourselves be Changed

Dogen says that *if you experience with your body the way insentient beings speak dharma, you will grasp with your body how all sages hear.* He calls this *the path of going beyond ordinary and going beyond sacred.* All phenomenal things have bodies that speak and hear. What we hear will not be what we expect to hear, so we may fail to notice it. *Insentient beings do not necessarily speak dharma with a voice heard by the ears.* It is not only grasses that hear in some other way than with eyes and ears, we also hear and respond in other ways. Grasping how all sages hear, we can hear in these ways too, with our wholehearted body-mind life, dropping off extraneous ideas of who is sentient and who is not.

The hallmark of hearing the dharma speaking of another being is that we are changed by the relationship. When we are changed by the impact of another being, by a stone that bruises a foot or a virus that invades the body, that is of course part of the dharma world of cause and effect, and we are affected by it. But that is not in itself hearing the dharma, because at that time we only know that being as an object causing us harm.

It is different when we pay attention to the being before us and reach toward connection. Seeing a white birch outside the window, our awareness draws us close to the tree, perhaps leading to a pleasurable sense of connection through the beauty it offers. Why then does Dogen say that only *foolish people may think that the sound of trees, or the opening and falling of leaves and flowers, is insentient beings speaking dharma?* He cautions against confusing appreciation of white birches or plum blossoms with hearing them speaking dharma, because appreciation operates on our terms. We look across the divide of self and other, and appreciate what we see on the basis of our values, thus reinforcing the gap dividing us from the delicate birch even as we reach across the divide. Esthetic enjoyment is a way of drawing close to the tree, but it does not extend to understanding the birch as the subject of its own life.

Appreciation can be a gateway beyond itself. When we feel gratitude for the grand, mysterious life of a redwood, we are changed by that gratitude, and there is a real relationship going on. If we are further moved to act on our gratitude, to preserve, restore, study those great beings, we receive further benefits. We are reminded of our place in the web of life, and get to participate in restoring our species to harmony with all the others. We are recalled to the opportunity to practice the bodhisattva precepts of restraint, which are a form of human dharma-speaking.

Another way we draw close to other people and other species is by projecting qualities onto them. We imbue whales and wolves with valor and patience, and we admire them for that. We think we see cowardly cunning in the fox among the chickens, and we feel justified to hunt it down. Projecting our inner movies on other people and other species (anthropomorphizing) has a bad reputation because we get so tangled up in it. It's a perfectly natural mental phenomenon, and it can be done sensitively and creatively, as when we try to feel our way into the life of another. In projection we reach farther across the divide between self and other than in appreciation, as we try out our ideas on the other. But we are still operating on our terms, and thus we are still reinforcing the divide as we reach across: this is *my* value I am seeing in you, whether you actually have that quality, or agree with me, or not.

Projection can be a gateway to real relationship when it carries a question with it. Remembering that it is our idea we are projecting on beings who are not a blank screen, we can carry a question with us as we reach out. We can ask how well our vision fits them, and what other quality would better express who they are. When we inquire about who they are from their side, what their life is like from their perspective, we are relating not just on our terms, but on theirs too, and we will be changed by the reality of the encounter.

Meeting another being in these ways, a subtle change of self-boundaries opens us to what is actually there, much as in zazen. A stammering, a flash of pleasure, a bright insight, a shiver—something in us is hearing the dharma speaking, because we are part of a dharma relationship and are willing and able to be changed by it. Often we experience this flash and shiver as gratitude or as intimacy, and we know we have received a gift.

We reach out toward other beings, and they toward us, across great divides of difference. With our sentience, we hear sentient voices. How do we hear insentient voices? Yunyan said, *"Insentient beings hear insentient beings speak dharma."* It is with our own insentient nature that we can hear insentient beings speak dharma. We have to study and verify our own sentient and insentient dharma nature, and our own dharma speaking. How do we verify that we are hearing trees and stones speak the dharma? By knowing how we are changed.

True encounters are ways of meeting without being stopped by differences. Zen is a practice of aiming at continuity—at dissolving the gaps and chasms between beings and between moments—and surrendering to life as it is. *The speaking never stops* and sometimes, when we are open to the intimacy of true meetings, we can hear it with our bodies, hearts, and minds, and be changed.

Does a Bomb Speak the Dharma?

All-inclusive dharma-speaking does not match human concepts of harmony and peace, posing endless conflicts for us. The dharma speaks of death as well as birth, of illness and loss as well as vigor, and the dharma says that the walls we build in our minds and lives to keep these apart are chimeras, empty of any firm reality. Dogen agrees with our sense that *the power of hearing dharma is not easy to know.* He reassures us that there is a way forward: *When we join the great assembly of buddha ancestors, and study their skin, flesh, bones, and marrow, there is no instant when the power of speaking dharma does not work.*

If a bobcat suddenly leaps up among the tall grasses when we are out walking, the chances are that our hearts will leap up in turn with pleasure at the appearance of this lively wild being. Noticing then a small, furry animal dangling from its mouth, we are likely to feel suddenly conflicted. Seeing life from one side and resting there, we are constantly brought up short.

Perhaps to be human is to be conflicted, because we have the capacity to see more than one point of view.

Most of us are now familiar with versions of the trolley-car dilemma that moral philosophers pose. If the trolley continues down its current track, several people will die; if the trolley is shunted to another track, a single person will die. You are outside watching the scene and have access to a lever that will shift the trolley to the other track. Will you do nothing (let things unfold, you didn't cause it, who are you to "play god") or will you intervene and send one person to death (assuming life and death power over others, taking responsibility to do what you think is the least harm through actively choosing someone's death)?

This is a stark and exaggerated dilemma, but the underlying issue of conflicting values comes up hundreds of times a day for each of us, with each choice we make. What's for breakfast? (How many of what kinds of beings are used or harmed in the making of my breakfast?) Shall we go to the movies? (Shall I consume limited resources for which people die and which contribute to climate change by driving my car to go see a movie?) The choices only get more complex: Shall I work longer hours than is right for my life, in order to benefit my family or my sangha? Many conflicts, like paradoxes, only apparently oppose each other, but threading our way through them is daunting.

It is inevitable and appropriate that we have a human-centered view of life and death, and within that, a personally centered view. But the dharma is not a view, and that is why it is so important. It is the encompassing reality of the ten-direction universe. Studying and practicing dharma, opening our eyes, flesh, and minds to hear and speak dharma, we can see even our own views as they are: by nature narrow, incomplete, and exclusionary.

The sixteen bodhisattva precepts that have been the core of Soto Zen ethics since Dogen are a bridge between the universal truth of dharma and the myriad phenomena of the dharma world that inevitably bump up against each other. The precepts are the time *when we join the great assembly of buddha ancestors, and study their skin, flesh, bones, and marrow.* The problem for us is that the dharma speaks in so many different individual voices. The resolution of the problem is that *there is no instant when the power of speaking dharma does not work.*

What about bombs and fracking? Are they the dharma speaking too? In this inclusive dharma universe, nothing is left out, not even weapons and strip mines. Take a bomb: it is made of various metals, each one innocently being itself. The ordinary crop fertilizer ammonium nitrate was made into the life-destroying bomb that tore apart the federal building in Oklahoma City. Ammonium nitrate became popular as a cheap and effective fertilizer because there was a lot of it left around after World War II, from materials stockpiled to make bombs. A full circle of cause and effect.

All natural ingredients are just "minding their own business," being themselves, humming their dharma songs, but then they are taken up and fashioned by us into weapons and iPads. We humans have some wisdom and a grand kind of consciousness, a great deal of it devoted to inventive ways of shaping things to suit ourselves. This industriousness of ours rests on a foundation of duality: of separation, opposition, and dominance. We prefer not to see this exclusionary foundation of our activities, but if we ignore it, we set a precedent for using these creations as weapons to conquer and kill. Denying the consequences of our acts and omissions, denying that all beings are our cousins, we wreak havoc and we deny ourselves, too. Acknowledging the sources and consequences of our actions, we can vow to pay attention, to take care, to adopt a high standard of accountability.

Speaking harm and speaking denial happen in the dharma world. Even weapons are the dharma speaking, but how hard it is to hear what they say, beyond our opinions of them. A bomb says, "Danger! Destruction!" and asks questions about our motives. A person who explodes a bomb is undoubtedly convinced he is right, that his view of the best outcome is correct. This is necessarily a fallacy, as no view is complete or absolutely right. Almost all aggression is experienced and justified as self-defense. A person doing harm as the way to do right is subject to a second great fallacy, too, the belief that the end justifies the means. The dharma says that is never the case: everything counts, everything is connected, nothing can be excluded. I personally cannot say that no violence is ever justified, but I know that there is little wisdom in it. I know, too, that none of us sees very widely and deeply, that all of us are clouded by narrow views.

Using the great elements, the amazing power of life, for our own ends regardless of the voices of others, we do tremendous harm. All forms of hatred and greed say, "I impose my will on you, I will not listen to your truth." Denial takes place within the dharma world, and it speaks dharma, but it does not speak dharma clearly. The voices of delusion speak of what happens when we deny the dharma of interwoven life. The dharma calls to us through this cacophony of delusive turmoil, crying out for us to wake up to who we are, to the world we really live in with all our cousins.

Living Together, Singing Together

Zazen is an activity of being awake to the speaking of myriad sentient and insentient beings. Even in zazen, this goes on largely beyond our consciousness, which could not contain or comprehend all this. But the speaking is never beyond our lives, our selves, and our actions. The dharma-speaking of all phenomena, so-called living and not living, fills the ten-direction universe. Dogen Zenji goes to great lengths to show us how it is that all beings are practicing and realizing together at all times and places, that all beings are actively singing the songs of dharma, and that the singing never stops.

Having received these great teachings, it is up to us to learn to attune our ears, eyes, bodies, and hands to hear and to make sense in our human way of the dharma speaking of all. True relationships with the many beings are essential for our own good and for the sake of all beings. If we do not do this, we risk damaging irreparably the world of all the beings inhabiting this spinning planet.

How do we extend the realm of our true relationships, deepening our already existing but so often misunderstood connections? At the close of his essay *Insentient Beings Speak Dharma*, Dogen says: *Know that insentient beings speaking dharma is the totality of buddha ancestors.* We can open ourselves to hearing this speaking, accept it as the voices of the buddha ancestors, and let ourselves be changed by it, so that we can live with confidence in terms of the truth of this inclusive dharma world.

Endnotes

(1) All quotes are from the work of Eihei Dogen, except one from *The Blue Cliff Record.*

(2) All quotes not specifically attributed are from "Insentient Beings Speak Dharma."

(3) Eihei Dogen. "Insentient Beings Speak Dharma"; "Valley Sounds, Mountain Colors"; and "Mountains and Waters Sutra." *Treasury of the True Dharma Eye: Zen Master Dogen's Shobo Genzo.* Vols. 1 and 2. Ed. Trans. Kazuaki Tanahashi. Boston: Shambhala, 2010.

(4) Quotes from *Shoakumakusa, Bendowa,* and *The Blue Cliff Record* are versions of the author's, Jisho Warner, unpublished.

UDUMBARA FLOWER

Udonge

Jan Chozen Bays

The udumbara flower, all beings love and enjoy it. (1, 2, 3)

Why would Dogen Zenji devote an entire fascicle of the *Shobogenzo* to praising a flower, a flower that some people say is mythical and does not exist? Others say it does exist, but it only blooms every 3,000 years, to herald the arrival of another Buddha, an enlightened being.

In modern times there are stories and photographs from Asia, of thousands of tiny white blossoms called udumbara flowers, mysteriously appearing on bricks, on buildings, on monuments, on grasses, and under a nun's laundry tub. Biologists say, no, these are not miraculous apparitions, they are simply the ordinary eggs of lacewing insects (4). Botanists counter that the udumbara is a *ficus*, a fig tree, different from *ficus religiosa*, the tree under which the Buddha was awakened.

This particular fig tree bears fruit very close to the trunk. They also say that it actually blooms all the time, but the flowers are hidden inside the fruit (5). In the *Shobogenzo* Dogen Zenji puts the udumbara flower in the hand of Shakyamuni Buddha, where it has the power to produce an enlightened being, smashing eyeballs and curving lips into a smile.

Each of these varied descriptions offer clues as to what the udumbara flower is. Is it non-existent, rare, or common? Does it flower continuously, hidden from our eyes, or does it bloom openly, for all to see, once in three millennia? These accounts of udumbara flowers seem contradictory, but in Zen we are intrigued, we are drawn in by contradictions and paradoxes. We begin to appreciate the weaving of the very fabric of our world out of the warp and woof of opposites, a world of delusion and enlightenment, of the impermanent and the deathless, of sacred and mundane, of the Unity and the Diversity. Dogen Zenji is at home in this world of apparent opposites. He is a mountain goat at play in the mountain range of paradox, happily leaping from peak to peak, jumping across huge chasms of apparent contradictions.

Dogen Zenji uses the udumbara flower to speak to us about enlightenment. *Holding up the flower is holding up the Buddha-mind,* he declares (6). He describes the udumbara flower in many ways, to help us understand what cannot be described in words, what can only be experienced directly by each individual for themselves. Dogen Zenji is speaking from his own experience of deep awakening, of the complete resolution of apparent opposites, using beautiful and evocative words. Let's investigate some of his words and the truths they point to.

Dogen Zenji writes, *The World Honored One held up an udumbara blossom and . . . said, 'I have the treasury of the true dharma eye . . .* ' (7). This word *treasury* means that the udumbara flower, the flower of enlightenment, is a treasure, an inheritance given to everyone, waiting to be taken up, owned and used. It is not diminished by being bestowed upon billions of beings. It is an inexhaustible treasure store, which *will open of itself [to] use as you will* (8).

We think of money and valuable possessions such as jewelry or cars as treasure. However, this is a false kind of treasure. It cannot buy happiness, wisdom, or ease of mind. Just look at the state of heart and mind of those who are considered wealthy, successful and honored, movie stars and wealthy financiers.

All Buddhas and their descendants *equally hold up this flower* (9). This word *equally* reassures us that no matter who we are, rich or poor, pale skinned or gleaming brown, articulate or silent, we each hold up the udumbara flower fully. Each one of us gets the entire bequest, so there is no ground for envy or strife. We are each the unique actualization of the Buddha Mind-and-Body at this very moment, in this very place.

It has never been lost (10). That it cannot be *lost* tells us that this flower is clearly visible and always present. It is each breath, each heartbeat, each hair, each eye blink, of every body; it is each leaf, stem and root tendril of every plant; it is the imperceptible disintegration of every mountain into every grain of sand beneath our feet. There is no place it does not exist, no place outside of it, so where is there a place for it to be lost? We also have never been lost. It is only when our mind grows confused or dark that we lose sight of it, like the sun disappearing temporarily behind storm clouds. Our practice is "eye medicine" to restore correct vision, and "mind medicine" to clear the mind ground, so that we can see and appreciate the continuous blooming of the udumbara flower for ourselves.

We must hold up the same flower (11). Dogen Zenji admonishes us to practice, to experience the same holding up of the *same flower* that Shakyamuni, Mahakasyapa, Dogen Zenji, and our own teachers did. *However this flower is holding up itself* (12). However, this flower does not need us to hold it up. It is continually held up. Out of this great flower everything in the world unfolds, a holy man in India, a cypress tree in China, a pebble in a cemetery, and you and me.

It is humans who divide this One Flower into five petals, eight stamens, *three vehicles, twelve schools, three sages and ten saints* (13). It is our ordinary mind that divides the world into categories, what we like and want more of or what we do not like and want to get rid of. It is this process of continually dividing, clinging and pushing away that obscures our pure, clear mind and prevents it from blooming and providing refreshment to those who inhabit a weary world.

It is beyond the understanding of (even the) . . . bodhisattvas (14). It is beyond the understanding of *anyone*. Although our minds *are* it, our minds cannot comprehend it, just like one cell that is the product of, functions within, and is intimate with, the entire body, but can never comprehend that body. Each ancestor has experienced the udumbara-flower nature and revealed it in a unique, irreproducible way, as each of us are doing now. Because it is everywhere, the gate to this blooming is always open. It is visible in the falling of pink petals, audible in a stone's strike, palpable in the grinding of a mortar, constantly given away in the movement of our bodies, constantly received in the touch of our clothing.

Holding up the flower existed before . . . . . during (and) . . . . . after the World Honored One attained enlightenment (15). The flower's life is eternal and it exists in all times and places at once. It exists before the Buddha of our time, during his life and forever afterward. At first startling to contemplate, this truth becomes comforting, because it means that our Enlightened Nature has always been, is, and always will be available, and thus can be experienced by anyone, any time, anywhere.

Arousing the aspiration for enlightenment and receiving initiation, as well as practice, realization, and continuation, all stir up the spring wind of holding up the flower (16). *The holding up of the flower . . . . .transcends time* (17). The time of our first awareness that enlightenment was possible, the time of our first step onto the path of practice, the time of our actual enlightenment and the time of our further practice all occur simultaneously. This means that as soon as we conceive of the possibility of enlightenment, we are enlightened. All the rest is "busy work." However, it may take a long time, even lifetimes. This is the identity of sudden and gradual enlightenment.

Shakyamuni conceals himself in the udumbara flower and yet reveals himself in the udumbara flower (18). Until we see it for ourselves, it is completely hidden, in plain sight. When we see it, it is seen everywhere. "So obvious," as my late master often exclaimed. When we see it, we also exclaim, "So obvious!" and its many costumes and disguises never fool us again.

I was moved by a recent photographic exhibit of homeless addicts in New York City (19). Their faces were ravaged. They supported life by selling scrap metal, drugs, and their bodies. Each one was happy that the photographer took the effort to take their picture and to talk to them. When asked what they wanted the people who passed them by all day to know about them, one said, " I am a good person with a good heart." Another said, " I'm just a person trying to get it right. I am caught in the grips but I am trying to get it right."

They are actually saying, "I am the Udumbara flower." The Udumbara blooms within the scarred face, the broken air conditioner being dragged on a leash down the street, the pendulous breasts of the middle aged prostitute in the red coat, the cardboard shelters that the street cleaners took away.

The coming and going of birth and death is a variety of blossom and their colors (20). It is like the largest organism in the world, an underground fungus that is 2,400 years old and covers 3.4 square miles (21). Walking around in the forest, we are unaware of this huge existence right under our feet. We only see its appearance above ground in the autumn when it blooms as a small mushroom here and there. Each birth, each death is the blooming of the udumbara flower, in its infinite variety of shapes and colors. The individual lives around us are what we are usually aware of, but they are just the visible manifestation of a Life of interconnection without boundaries. There is always more to see.

All beings love and enjoy it (22). Our own life is the flowering of Life; we should love our life and enjoy it. We get one chance to savor each bite of food. We get one chance to savor each moment of our life. How can we truly taste and enjoy it?

"When Gautama's eyeball is smashed . . . (23). Smashing an eyeball sounds violent, but more violent are the consequences of retaining the intact eyeball that sees "I am here looking at you over there." When we look through this eyeball, we can become angry or afraid of people whose skin or hairstyle or dress look different from ours. When I look at people with dread locks I am grateful to my son. Because he was a Rastafarian for a while, people who have dreads don't look strange to me. They look like my son. Instead of being anxious when I encounter them on a dark street, I can smile. And they can smile back.

On various people's faces hang Gautama's eyes, but still they beat their breasts with fists in empty grieving (24). When we cannot see with the Buddha's eyes, we are dissatisfied. We seem to have enough, but we know that something is missing. When suddenly we see through the Buddha's eyes, we see that everything is star-bright and blooming perfectly. Grief for the world dissolves, our hearts open and our lips naturally curve into a smile. *His face immediately changes and is replaced with the face of taking up the flower (25).*

Our eyeball is immediately smashed . . . (26). When we sit in zazen and "think of non-thinking," the notions of time and space, self and other that are intricately embedded in our mind are loosened. If we sit long and deep enough, they disappear. Then we look at "our" hand with wonder, as it raises a spoon, a hoe or a flower. When the flower is held up everything, hand-eye-flower, participates in one complete activity. At the time of holding up there is no difference in time or space between the Buddha, Mahakasyapa, Dogen Zenji and us. *At the very moment of taking up the flower, all Gautamas, all Mahakasyapas, all sentient beings, all of us hold up a single hand and together take up the flower (27).* All the ancestors manifest here and now, in our activity of sitting on the cushion, chanting, bowing and holding up our *oryoki* bowls. Shakyamuni Buddha holds up the flower, Dogen Zenji holds up the flower, I write and you read. I will smile as I write it if you will smile as you read it. We should enjoy all these as the activities of holding up.

When you take up 'I have' and replace it with entrusting, you uphold the treasury of the true dharma eye (28). This is the moment of transmission, when the "I have" of "my" small body and mind drops away. We are catapulted into the huge Dharma body and vast Buddha mind, which become our permanent refuge. We trust, it entrusts.

Further our entire body becomes the hand holding up the flower (29). The activity of our bodies, putting on robes, sitting, breathing, walking, bowing, chanting, cooking, cleaning, is the twirling of the flower, the turning of the dharma wheel. This is the way the practice of the ancients is held up so that future generations can recognize and enjoy it.

The most important thing is . . . complete and undivided attention. If you can manifest this spirit when you make a prostration in the Buddha Hall or practice zazen in the monastery the flower of your mind will become more brilliant and the things around you will become more beautiful (30). When zazen clears our mind's eye, everything becomes more brilliant and beautiful. When we observe this we should realize that this is not an extraordinary condition. It is the way things actually are.

When Shakyamuni lost his ordinary vision it was like a single branch of a plum tree blooming in the snow. Soon after the plum blossoms were in full bloom, tiny branches appeared all over. Instead of wondering about this people should laugh at the spring wind blowing wildly (31). In our monastery garden we encountered a few old plum trees. Over decades of neglect they had dropped fruit that grew into a dense thicket of thorny, vigorous young trees. Thus one branch of blossoms became a forest with many branches, spreading everywhere. We thinned those trees into rows, so they have more light and air. When the wind blows, plum blossoms fall and you can see the small green fruits forming amidst the thorns.

The opening of peach blossoms is stimulated by the spring wind (32). Here Dogen Zenji talks of the openings caused by the spring wind. Elsewhere he says, *The wind of Buddhism actualizes the gold of the earth and turns its long river into sweet cream* (33). Gold is worthless until it is extracted from the earth and refined. Even then it is only given worth by human interchange. Our practice has the ability to reveal the gold within the rich earth of our life, and to refine our life into something of benefit to ourselves and everyone we encounter. Where can we find this miraculous wind of Buddhism? We need only to open our minds to it. It is generated by our every breath, by our bows, by our robes as we walk in *kinhin*. This wind stimulates the opening of blossoms of all kinds, blossoms that will drop off over and over, producing fruit that ripens now and continuously for all eternity. This is the wind that ripens the life of each one of us into sweet fruit that can be enjoyed by all.

The udumbara flower inside of each of us calls us to practice, to sit, to chant, to translate, to be born, and to die, so that it can bloom. Over and over, over and over, the udumbara flower appears and disappears, as the millions of insect eggs hidden in the leaves in our gardens, as the millions of people on our planet, as the millions of fiery suns encircled by planets inhabited by unknown life that are hidden in our Universe. The udumbara flower blooms as the mysterious shining being that has your name.

Dogen Zenji calls us not just to read about the udumbara flower, but to directly realize it, to seize the rare and precious opportunity to practice, so that we can experience for ourselves the unfolding of its creamy petals and the subtle scent of its blooming in our unique life. The udumbara flower, may all beings enjoy and love it!

Endnotes

(1) This essay uses two translations of the fascicle about the udumbara flower in the *Shobogenzo*, (2) and (6) below. There are a number of other translations in English, but it is a vertiginous task to consult them all, one that I hope to save all but the most meticulous reader. The translation by Nishiyama and Stevens was the first that was available to me as a young Zen student, and it made a deep impression. The translation by Tanahashi is the most recent to appear and its poetry is inspiring a new generation.

(2) Eihei Dogen. "Udumbara Blossom." *Treasury of the True Dharma Eye: Zen Master Dogen's Shobogenzo.* Ed. Trans. Kazuaki Tanahashi. Boston: Shambhala, 2010. 642-645.

(3) Dogen Zenji takes these words from the second chapter of the *Lotus Sutra*. " It is like the udumbara flower which all the world loves and delights in, which heavenly and human beings look on as something rare, but which appears only once in many, many ages." *The Lotus Sutra.* Trans. Burton Watson. NY: Columbia University Press, 1883. 45.

(4) For photos and a video of "udumbara flowers" appearing in Asia see:
Preuss, Simone. In Search of the Flower That Blooms Every 3,000 Years. Environmental Graffiti website, 2012. <http://www.environmentalgraffiti.com/featured/in-search-of-the-flower-that-blooms-every-3000-years/12623?image=0 >
For the botanists' view see these on-line articles, 2012.
http://en.wikipedia.org/wiki/Udumbara_%28Buddhism%29
and http://www.khandro.net/nature_trees.htm

(5) Ibid.

(6) Eihei Dogen. "Udonge: The flower of an udumbara tree." *Dogen Zenji's Shobogenzo: The Eye and Treasury of the True Law.* Trans. Kosen Nishiyama and John Stevens. Sendai, Japan: Daihokkaikaku Publishing Company, 1975. 117-120.

(7) Tanahashi, 642.

(8) Bielefeldt, Carl. " Principles of Seated Meditation." *Dogen's Manuals of Zen Meditation.* Berkeley: University of California Press, 1988. 174-187.

(9)   Tanahashi, 642.

(10) Nishiyama and Stevens, 117.

(11) Ibid.

(12) Ibid.

(13) Ibid.

(14) Tanahashi, 643.

(15) Tanahashi, 643. Nishiyama and Stevens, 118.

(16) Tanahashi, 643.

(17) Nishiyama and Stevens, 118.

(18) Ibid.

(19) Arnade, Chris. Faces of Addiction, Flicker site. 2012. http://www.flickr.com/photos/arnade/sets/72157627894114489.

(20) Tanahashi, 643.

(21) Casselman, Anne. Strange but True: The Largest Organism on Earth Is a Fungus. *Scientific American* online. October 4, 2007.   http://www.scientificamerican.com/article.cfm?id=strange-but-true-largest-organism-is-fungus.

(22) Tanahashi, 644.

(23) Ibid., 645.

(24) Eihei Dogen. *Dogen's Extensive Record: A Translation of the Eihei Koroku.* Trans. Taigen Dan Leighton and Shohaku Okumura. Boston: Wisdom, 2004. 174.

(25) Tanahashi, 644.

(26) Ibid.

(27) Tanahashi, 644.

(28) Ibid.

(29) Nishiyama and Stevens, 119.

(30) Ibid.

(31) Ibid.

(32) Tanahashi, 645.

(33) Eihei Dogen. " Genjo Koan: Manifesting Absolute Reality," *Sound of Valley Streams: Enlightenment in Dogen's Zen.* Trans. Francis H. Cook. Albany, NY: SUNY, 1989. 65-69.

WORKS CONSULTED IN INTRODUCTION AND BRIEF BIOGRAPHY

Arai, Paula Kane Robinson. *Women Living Zen*. NY: Oxford Univ. Press, 1999.

Cabezon, Jose Ignacio. *Buddhism, Sexuality, and Gender*. Albany: SUNY Press, 1992.

Carney, Eido Frances. "Dogen's View of Women." Presentation at the Zen Translation Forum, San Francisco Zen Center, 2010. Portions of the Introduction were delivered at this event honoring the publication of Kazuaki Tanahashi's translation of *Shobogenzo*.

Dogen's Extensive Record A Translation of the Eihei Koroku. Trans. Taigen Dan Leighton and Shohaku Okumura. Boston: Wisdom Publications, 2004.

Eihei Dogen. *Fukanzazengi*. Trans. Soto Shu Shumucho. Tokyo: Japan, 1986.

—. *Shobogenzo*. Trans. Hubert Nearman. Mt. Shasta, CA: Shasta Abbey Press, 2007.

—. *Enlightenment Unfolds The Essential Teachings of Zen Master Dogen*. Ed. Kazuaki Tanahashi. Boston: Shambhala, 1999.

Johnson, Allan G. *Privilege, Power, and Difference.* NY: McGraw-Hill, 2001.

Kim, Hee-Jin. *Eihei Dogen Mystical Realist.* Somerville, MA: Wisdom Publications, 2004.

Kodera, Takashi James. *Dogen's Formative Years in China, An Historical Study and Annotated Translation of the Hokyo-ki.* Boulder, CO: Prajna Press, 1980.

Schireson, Grace. *Zen Women, Beyond Tea-Ladies, Iron Maidens, and Macho Masters.* Boston: Wisdom, 2009.

Yokoi, Yuho. *Zen Master Dogen.* New York: Weatherhill, 1976.

GLOSSARY OF TERMS
FOUND IN THE ESSAYS

Bodhicitta is a Sanscrit word which refers to the awakened mind or the mind of enlightenment. It also means the seed of awakening which is nurtured by the intention to practice and the actualization of practice in the heart of compassion.

Bodhisattva means an "enlightenment being," a helper who practices virtue, resides in the nature of compassion and wisdom, and assists other beings in the steps toward liberation. The bodhisattva promises to remain as a helper to alleviate suffering and foregoes nirvana until all beings are awakened. Bodhisattva can also mean a personification of Buddha Nature

Bodhi-Mind is the mind of wisdom awakened in the unity of subject and object, and realization of the essential nature of emptiness of all existence. The awakened mind also refers to realization and insight of the four noble truths.

Buddha-Dharma, in Zen, is the ungraspable truth, which rests in the enlightenment experience of Shakyamuni

Buddha, which we too grasp in our experience of awakening. It is not transmitted orally or through texts, but rather is realized in the direct experience of awakening in every moment.

Buddha Nature is the true and eternal nature of all sentient life. This means that through appropriate spiritual practice all sentient life may experience the realization of enlightenment and buddhahood.

Dharma has numerous meanings: that which is the underlying nature of the world; the teachings or the law of universal truth; all living phenomena; the ethical rules of behavior for Buddhist practitioners; a reflection of the content of the human mind.

Dharmakaya, in Mahayana Buddhism, is one of "three bodies" that express the absolute dynamic of a Buddha: the Dharmakaya (transcendent reality); Sambhogakaya (the enjoyment of truth); Nirmanakaya (the earthly body of transformation). Dharmakaya is essentially the true spiritual nature of Buddha, beyond duality and without characteristics.

Emptiness in Buddhism means that inherent existence is dependently originated in all its causes and conditions even in the principle of causality. Emptiness is therefore pure mind, the mind of enlightenment.

Gassho is a gesture of unity and supplication made with the hands, holding them palm-to-palm and upright in front of the body and away from the face. It signifies a sign of courtesy and greeting between Buddhists, and is used formally in religious ceremony as a sign of reverence.

Genzo-e is a special study retreat to investigate the teachings of Eihei Dogen.

Kensho is a Japanese word that means, "seeing one's nature." Sometimes this is synonymous with *satori*, which means the experience of awakening or enlightenment. It is the experience that cannot be explained or grasped conceptually as it is beyond duality and beyond seeing oneself as a self. *Kensho* also implies an "opening" experience that is still to be deepened through continual practice.

Kesa or *Okesa* is a large patchwork robe most often made of humble cloth that is worn by Zen priests for Zazen and ceremony. During other occasions in the monastery, the *rakusu*, or little robe, will be worn. As a special celebration, more elaborate robes made of richer cloth may be worn.

Koan is a paradoxical teaching, phrase, or brief narrative used in Zen training to direct the mind toward the nature of ultimate reality. A koan cannot be answered or understood through reason, but requires an insight or intuitive leap that takes one beyond logical mentation to another level of understanding.

Lotus Sutra, that is, a discourse of the Buddha, was delivered toward the end of his public life that contains the complete teachings of the Buddha. In this sutra, the Buddha is not a historical figure, but rather a transcendent Nature, available to everyone such that they themselves can awaken to their own True Nature and become a Buddha themselves.

Mudra is a way of holding the hands or the body in a symbolic gesture to indicate an aspect of the Buddha.

All Buddhist iconography contains a particular gesture of the hands to point toward a significant aspect such as protection, care of the Sutras, supreme wisdom, concentration, fearlessness, or a myriad of other spiritual expressions.

Nirvana, in Zen, is synonymous with Buddha nature or with prajna, wisdom. When one has attained prajna, that is, awakening into one's true nature, then one lives in the state of Nirvana, which is not separate from this existence. Nirvana is the state of living one's true nature as a human being.

Oryoki refers first to the nesting bowls that one receives during ordination and which will be the only religious "property" of a Zen monk along with the robe. Today, lay people also receive *oryoki* bowls. Another meaning refers simply to the one bowl that the Buddha's followers used for their begging rounds and meals. A third meaning is the ceremony of meal taking during which practitioners eat in silence and handle the bowls in a formal, ceremonial way. The word *oryoki* in Japanese means "holding just enough" which implies that one eats without greed and takes just enough to meet the body's need for nutrition and energy for the work one is doing.

Rakusu means, "little robe" and is a rectangular religious article worn by priests, monks, and lay people to symbolize the patchwork robe of Shakyamuni Buddha. It is made of cloth and is conferred on someone who takes the Precepts and is initiated into Buddhism.

Sangha is one of the Three Treasures: Buddha, Dharma, and Sangha. The Sangha is the Buddhist community of practitioners. In a monastery, or in the original Buddhist community, sangha may refer only to those who are practicing monks, whereas in a wider sense, it includes all who are equally practicing together.

Satori (see also Kensho) may be synonymous with *kensho*, but is often referred to as the Buddha's or the Matriarchal/Patriarchal Ancestors' great awakening, while *Kensho* is an initial beginning awakening or enlightenment experience.

Sesshin means to "gather or collect the heart-mind." It is a time of intense Zazen with the whole heart-mind engaged fully in practice. In a monastery, *sesshin* may occur several times a month lasting one week at a time. In Zen centers, *sesshin* may be less frequent, but the intention of full engagement of the heart-mind in Zazen is the same.

Skanda is a collection of traits or aggregates that form what we might call the human personality. They include, form, feeling, perception, thoughts, and consciousness. These aggregates by themselves are impermanent, empty, and without essence. Nevertheless, they are the cause or the object of attraction to appetite, longing, or desire, which brings about suffering. As there is no true abiding "self" there is no real personality or ego to be found and thus, the "ego self" is an illusion.

Shikantaza, *shikan* means "only this;" *ta* means "precisely;" *za* means, "to sit." It means to forego techniques of meditation and instead, to practice what is called Zazen: a state of attentive, bright awareness, and being present to everything equally without directing the mind toward any particular object.

Shravaka is a student in search of enlightenment who can experience this only by "hearing" the Buddha's teachings and realizing the essence of the four noble truths. The *Shravaka* is one who has Nirvana as an ultimate goal.

Shugyo refers to deep, focused, mind-body training that engages right effort and mindfulness in activity, such as Zazen, that leads to liberation. While monastic training is referred to as *shugyo*, all activity of a Zen practitioner, whether monk or layperson, is undertaken mindfully. The work of a householder or a business person can lead to the opening of the mind and full presence when the activities of daily life are not frivolous, but they are spiritual activities in their true context as the means to liberation.

Vinaya translates as the "Basket of Discipline" which contains the rules and regulations governing the community of monks and nuns and essentially regulates the moral, ethical, and spiritual aspects for daily life of those who live in the monastic Vinaya rule.

Zazen means seated attentiveness in an actively present state, attentive to each passing moment, without focusing on any particular object or thought. This is also called *shikantaza*, or just sitting, which is the practice of being one's true self, or Buddha nature.

Zen simply means meditation. Today is has taken on many connotations, some of them appropriated to seem part of an in-group or faddish connection, however Zen is a sacred practice that begins with Zazen, meditation. It is inappropriate to apply the word "Zen" to frivolous or banal uses. Za means to sit and Zen means to meditate. There is no Zen without Zazen.

Zendo is a hall or room set aside for the practice of Zazen. While monasteries have formal designs for the arrangement of monks and practitioners, one may also set up a less formal zendo in one's home or office, embracing the practice of Zazen in daily life.

CONTRIBUTORS

Shosan Victoria Austin

Austin is a Soto Zen priest in her fortieth year of practice at San Francisco Zen Center and Tassajara Zen Mountain Monastery. She was Dharma Transmitted by Sojun Mel Weitsman Roshi, abbot of the Berkeley Zen Center. She is a yoga teacher and former president of San Francisco Zen Center. She has written and published articles in various Buddhist magazines.

Jan Chozen Bays

Co-abbot and co-founder of Great Vow Monastery in the White Plum lineage, she is a pediatrician specializing in child abuse. She helped found CARES NW, a child abuse clinic in Portland and has lectured throughout the US and abroad. She is author of *Jizo Bodhisattva: Guardian of Children, Travelers, and Other Voyagers; Mindful Eating: A Guide To Rediscovering A Healthy And Joyful Relationship With Food; How to Train a Wild Elephant: And Other Adventures in Mindfulness.*

Eido Frances Carney

Beginning practice in 1971 with Kobun Chino Otogawa Roshi, she received Dharma Transmission from Niho Tetsumei Roshi in 1997 at Entsuji Temple, in lineage with the hermit priest Ryokan after training at Shoboji Temple in Japan. She has since founded Olympia Zen Center in Washington, and served as president of the national Soto Zen Buddhist Association. She was adjunct faculty in Humanities for ten years at South Puget Sound Community College. In 2006, her teacher named her Abbess of Fukujuji Temple in Nakasho, Japan. She promotes the teaching and poetry of Ryokan, has lectured in the U.S. and abroad, and is a published writer, poet and painter.

Shotai De La Rosa

Shotai is the Head Priest at Daishin Zendo in Hialeah, Florida where she lives. Her practice began in Bogotá, Colombia in 1989 and she went on to train with Rev. Dokusho Villalba at the Luz Serena Temple in Spain from 1990 to 1992. After training at Luz Serena Temple, she practiced in Italy with Rev. Fausto Taiten Guareschi at Shobozan Fudenji from 1992-1997. In 1998, she continued her study and practice at the San Francisco Zen Center. In 2004, she moved to Sanshin Zen Community and from 2006 to 2007 she trained at the Aichi Senmon Nisodo in Japan. She received the title of *kyoshi* from the Headquarters of the Soto Zen in Japan in 2007. She is today a member of the Soto Zen Buddhist Association. Shotai focuses her practice in zazen (*shikantaza*) as undefiled and formless sitting and the cultivation of the wisdom and compassion of the Buddha.

Teijo Munnich.

Disciple and Dharma heir of Dainin Katagiri Roshi, Munnich studied with him from 1975 until his death in 1990. She received formal training at Hokyoji (Catching the Moon Zen Mountain Center) in Minnesota, Tassajara Zen Mountain Center in California, and Hosshinji in Obama, Japan. In addition to her work in developing Great Tree, Munnich is Dharma teacher for the Zen Center of Asheville and Charlotte Zen Meditation Society in Charlotte, North Carolina. From Catholic Convent, to life on the road, to a university education and time spent as a dancer, Munnich has spent the last 30 years as a Zen Buddhist monk.

Josho Pat Phelan

The Chapel Hill Zen Center in North Carolina, in the Spring of 1991, invited Phelan to move to NC to lead the group. Phelan was ordained in 1977 by the former Abbot of the San Francisco Zen Center, Zentatsu Richard Baker, who was Suzuki Roshi's successor. She has also studied with two of Suzuki Roshi's other disciples, Sojun Mel Weitsman and Tenshin Reb Anderson. In addition, she practiced with Robert Aitken Roshi of the Diamond Sangha in Hawaii. Prior to her arrival in Chapel Hill in August, 1991, she was a Practice Leader and Director of Zen Center's residence facility in San Francisco. In 1995, Phelan received Dharma Transmission from Sojun Mel Weitsman and was installed as Abbess of the CHZC in 2000. She performed Zuise in Japan in 2008.

Byakuren Judith Ragir

Ragir is the guiding teacher at Clouds in Water Zen Center. She studied with Dainin Katagiri Roshi from

1973-1990 at the Minnesota Zen Meditation Center in Minneapolis. Following his death in 1990, Ragir was instrumental in founding the Clouds in Water Zen Center in St. Paul, and in 2006 became the guiding teacher. In December 2007, she received Dharma Transmission from Joen Snyder–O'Neal in Katagiri Roshi's lineage.

Shinshu Roberts

Shinshu Roberts is ordained in the Soto Zen lineage of Shunryu Suzuki Roshi and received Dharma Transmission from Sojun Weitsman Roshi, Abbot of the Berkeley Zen Center. She holds the appointment of Kokusaifukyoshi (teacher qualification) with the administrative headquarters of Soto Zen in Japan. Rev. Roberts and Rev. Daijaku Kinst are co-founders and teachers at Ocean Gate Zen Center in Capitola, CA.

Seisen Saunders

Saunders is the founder and head teacher of Sweetwater Zen Center. She was a student of the late Taizan Maezumi Roshi and a Dharma successor of Roshi Bernie Glassman, cofounder of the Greyston Mandala and the Zen Peacemaker Order. Saunders lived at the Zen Center of Los Angeles for 15 years, and worked on ZCLA's administrative staff. She served for four years as the co-abbot of Yokoji Zen Mountain Center, a traditional monastery and practice center in Idyllwild, California.

Grace Jill Schireson

Founder and Abbess of the Empty Nest Zen Group, Modesto Valley Heartland Zen Group, and the Fresno

River Zen Group, Schireson is a Dharma heir in the lineage of Shunryu Suzuki Roshi. She is President of the Shogaku Zen Institute, a seminary for Zen sangha leaders. She is author of the book *Zen Women: Beyond Tea Ladies, Iron Maidens and Macho Masters.* She trained with Sojun Mel Weitsman Roshi from whom she received Dharma transmission in 2005, and Mountain Seat Ceremony in 2009. Schireson also trained in Rinzai Zen in Japan under Keido Fukushima Roshi, former abbot of Tofuku-ji Monastery in Kyoto. She is a clinical psychologist and has taught classes on Zen throughout the United States.

Jisho Warner

Warner is a Soto Zen priest, and the guiding teacher and founder of Stone Creek Zen Center in Sonoma County, California. A former president of the Soto Zen Buddhist Association, Warner trained for many years both in Japan and the United States. Having graduated from Harvard University in 1965, she was also a longtime student of Dainin Katagiri. Warner was editor for several prominent Buddhist writers and scholars. She is part of the translator-editor team of the book *Opening the Hand of Thought* by Kosho Uchiyama. She practiced for many years at the Milwaukee Zen Center under Tozen Akiyama, from whom she received Dharma Transmission.

Made in the USA
Charleston, SC
04 February 2013